SCHOOL LEADERSHIP

SCHOOL LEADERSHIP

Learner-Centered Leadership in Times of Crisis

TOM BUTLER, PH.D.

BUTLER LEADERSHIP CONSULTING LLC

This book is available at special discounts when purchased in quantity for educational purposes. For inquiries and details, contact the author at tom@poweringuped.com

Published by Butler Leadership Consulting, LLC
www.butlerleadershipconsulting.com

Edited by Jessica Shrout

Cover design by Susan Malikowski
Interior design by Phillip Gessert
Graphics by Chris Davis

School Leadership: Learner-Centered Leadership in Times of Crisis; by Tom Butler, Ph.D.

Paperback ISBN: 978-1-7360032-0-6
Ebook ISBN: 978-1-7360032-1-3

DEDICATION

To Kim, Emma, Anna, and Richie

"Next in importance to freedom and justice is popular education, without which neither freedom nor justice can be permanently maintained."

—James A. Garfield

TABLE OF
CONTENTS

LIST OF
FIGURES

ACKNOWLEDGMENTS

S CHOOL LEADERSHIP WOULD not exist without the friendship, mentorship, and coaching from colleagues and friends throughout my career. Early in my career, Michael G. Schwarz, Jim Eagen, Diana Barnes, Dan Stevens, Wayne Crawford, and Mrs. Bellamy helped set my career course on becoming learner-centered. I also want to thank Pat Crawford, Duff Rearick, Jay Scott, Arnold Hillman, and Mike Vereb, for taking the time to push my thinking and always encouraging me to stay focused on kids. A special thank you to Brent and Gelaine Rhoads for guiding me through my first superintendency. I have been blessed to work with outstanding leaders during my career. For all of the leaders I worked with at the Northern Tioga School District, the Ridgway Area School District, the Penn Trafford School District, and Appalachia Intermediate Unit 8, I thank you for shaping my thinking and constantly reminding me about what is important in education.

INTRODUCTION

"TOM, CAN YOU believe what the State Department of Education expects us to do now? It's not bad enough that schools have been closed by order of the Governor, they want us to...." Since the middle of March, when schools across Pennsylvania and the United States were closed, I have had many conversations with school leaders that started just like the example above. The Federal government, the State government, and the local school board expect school leaders to have "the answer" to all the complex situations that have arisen since the COVID-19 virus upended the education world. If we are not careful, we will find ourselves ping-ponging from one crisis decision to another. Long-term, strategic planning for the school district gets set aside as we focus on short-term survival.

Now is not the time to throw in the towel and forget about our leadership responsibilities. All of us got into education to help students. We got into school leadership so we could help lead schools and school districts. We know how to do this under normal circumstances. We all know that we are not living in normal circumstances right now, but we can take everything that we have learned in our leadership journey and apply it to the crisis we now face. In fact, this is the perfect opportunity to put that training into action. Let's take a step back and reflect on our current situation, and devise ways to leverage the chaos to help our students and schools.

The goal of this book is to assist you by offering a framework of leadership that can help you find your leverage points in your school or school district. The core tenet of School Leadership is something I call radically learner-centered. Radically learner-centered education happens when all decisions throughout the school organization are made through the lens of each individual learner. The New Learning Ecosystem is a simple structure to help you contextualize how to become radically learner-centered.

It assists you in creating conditions within the school system that helps you focus on the essential part of school: the learners.

This book tells the story of how school leaders can navigate a crisis. The characters, situations, and settings are fictional—but you may have run into them before in your own district. In many ways, this book is about crisis leadership. My goal in writing this book is to offer you a way to reflect on your specific challenges and use those challenges to springboard your school district to a post-COVID-19 world where the students benefit—one where we're not just surviving, but thriving. In my experience, when school leaders, and leadership teams, focus on what is best for learners, better outcomes occur for everyone. The good news? It's inexpensive to make the changes outlined in this book—you do not need a consultant. You can take the principles and suggestions in this book and implement them yourself—and many have already done it! Ultimately, you can help your students and schools thrive because of the COVID-19 crisis. This book will help you get there. Good luck!

Here are some tips to help you navigate the book.

1. Interjected throughout the story are shadow boxes that provide clarity for the reader on vocabulary or critical topics. There are three purposes for the boxes:

    a. To define terms (Definition)
    b. To give my opinion (My Two Cents)
    c. To highlight key quotes within the book (Quotes)

2. At the end of each chapter is a resource section that directs the leader to books, articles, and web resources that are relevant to the topics discussed in the chapter. The resource list is not meant to exhaustive, but it will help interested readers in furthering their knowledge of the topics discussed.

3. Each chapter ends with discussion questions. The questions are meant to spur conversations within a school district's leadership team or professional learning community. Along the way, these conversations will help your school or school district become more learner-centered. Use the questions with

leadership team book studies, among colleagues, and in graduate classes.

Use this book to start conversations within your school community on how your school or school district can become radically learner-centered. Conduct a book study with your leadership team, your PTA, your school board, or your faculty and start reimagining learning in a post-COVID-19 world.

PROLOGUE
MARCH 2020

ROB, THE SUPERINTENDENT of schools, looks around the corner to where his kitchen used to be. The walls are down to the studs, just like they should be at this point in the project—at least, that's what the contractor is saying. Living with a kitchen that's just studs is an entirely different matter. The living room is stripped down to studs and joists, too. Everything is exactly as it should be...or is it? He walks out to his garage, which is now the living room, and grabs the keys to his car. He sighs, looking at his sofa squeezed up against the family's bicycles with DVDs precariously stacked on its cushions. It's going to be like this for a while. Construction is on hold and wishful thinking will not bring back the first floor of his house.

During the drive to his office, Rob ponders the similar course his school district is on. The day before, the county went under a "stay at home order" because of the COVID-19 pandemic. When his contractor arrived to work the next day, he had barely hooked on his tool belt when local law enforcement came to the worksite and told him his work was not deemed "essential," and he had to go home. "What can you do? We will just have to make the best of it," Rob thought.

Luckily, he's had plenty to keep his mind occupied. For the past two weeks, Rob has been busy transitioning his school district from a brick and mortar traditional school to a virtual school. The shock to his school occurred on a Friday (the 13TH no less!) when the Governor closed all the school buildings in his State. Overnight, Rob's best-laid plans of schooling and education changed. No more busses, sporting events, or band concerts. Well, not for now, anyway. These concerns changed to internet accessibility for his students, lunch programs for families, and training all his teachers in one week how to adapt their lesson plans to teach online. Pulling into the parking lot to his office, Rob thinks that if he can figure out all that stuff at work, he can figure out how to live with no functional first floor of his house.

Rob walks through what's normally a bustling workplace to get to his office. He sits down at his desk and tries to ignore the buzzing on his cell phone, announcing emails and text messages. Leading schools in a time of crisis is a challenge. Schools are such an integral part of the lives of the community, and a crisis exposes how much the school is woven into the fabric of the community. Parents are now looking for childcare; bus contractors can't pay their drivers; sporting events are canceled. It's as if someone pulled on a thread of the community fabric and the entire piece unraveled. When a severe crisis occurs, the community looks to schools for safety and stability—a challenge Rob recognizes and welcomes.

Rob knows his community well. After all, the job of a school superintendent requires that you be engrained in the community. He knows that throughout their lives, community members have counted on the school to be "there." Maybe they did not agree with everything the school has done or felt angry with personnel from the school at times, but the school was omnipresent. Rob's learned that schools are a lot like family... "locals" can criticize it themselves, but if someone outside the community criticizes it, watch out! During the first days of the COVID-19 crisis, the physical presence of the school was gone. The hub of the community was taken away.

Rob thinks back on all the books he has read about leadership theory over the years. He chuckles at some of the experiences he has had as a superintendent, some that went well, and some that did not go so well (who can forget the notorious firing of the football coach). He wonders how this combination of theory and practical experience can help him as he navigates the COVID-19 crisis.

Thinking too much about all the problems starts to overwhelm him, so Rob decides to go for a walk. Rob's office is in an elementary school and walking through an empty hallway to the exit is disorienting and chaotic. Usually, at this time of the day, he is fending off kids that want to give him a hug, or teachers that want him to answer a burning question right now. He used to get annoyed at these interruptions but now longs for them. "Oh well," he tells himself, "I need some fresh air and a fresh perspective to help me figure out where to start to lead the school and the community during this mess."

He steps outside and quickly finds the trailhead to the nature path that surrounds the school. He drinks it in: the stillness, the silence, the sounds of birds in the trees. Have they always been here? The lack of human noise feels like an echo. "The benefit of being an 'essential' employee means I can be out here by myself," Rob thinks to himself. He stops and listens to the distinctive sound of a red-winged blackbird perched on a nearby fencepost. His focus on the bird makes the surrounding environment disappear. He sees and hears only the bird. It's as if the problems overwhelming Rob vanished from his mind for one blissful moment. The bird doesn't pay any attention to Rob. He's solely focused on calling for a mate. "How simple," Rob thinks. "How freeing it must be to have the drive and singular focus of this bird."

The bird finishes his song and flutters away, but he leaves Rob with a gift...the gift of clarity. Rob smiles to himself as he turns around on the path and heads back to his office. "It's funny how the brain works. Sometimes you must stop trying so hard to find a solution and allow your brain the space to work without distractions. Now I've got my game plan!"

Rob starts to outline his plan on the way back to his office. "We must stay true to learners, stay true to ourselves, and stay true to staff in this crisis. If we just concentrate on those three things, we will become a better school when the COVID-19 crisis, or any crisis we have in the future, decides to come into our communities."

Stepping out of the trailhead, Rob considers his new three pillars. In a sense, "staying true" is more than a way to lead through a crisis. The pillars are a framework for leading a school at any time. The education world is filled with so much noise around reform and innovation. Outside experts are constantly telling teachers, principals, and superintendents how to do their job. Rob believes these well-meaning school reformers have de-professionalized educators. He thinks of curriculums that are implemented where teachers literally read from a script to their learners. Policies made at the State and Federal level that limit the budgetary options of school leaders is another example of interference. Finally, the confusion around education leadership with too many voices (often conflicting) offering the best way forward muddies the waters even more.

STAYING TRUE TO LEARNERS

STAYING TRUE SIMPLIFIES school leadership. There are so many aspects of the job that you cannot control that we need to remind ourselves of the things we can control.

> ## STAYING TRUE TO YOUR LEARNERS
>
> Staying true to your learners occurs when the entire system of schooling is designed, and operates, in the best interest of every individual learner.

We can control staying true to our learners. After all, learners are the only reason schools exist. In Rob's view, there seems to be an "education industrial complex" that continually churns out recommendations, policies, and research whose unintended consequence is the complication of the learning process. Placing all the recommendations, policies, and research in the proper context is an essential facet of "staying true to learners."

Rob stops midway through the parking lot and looks over at the bus garage. Generally, at this time of the day, the bus garage would be busy with busses coming and going from their student runs. Now, all the busses sit empty. He feels a pang of longing to have those busses full of students again. While we wait for them to return to school, what can the district be doing to stay true to learners?

School leaders have a unique perspective on their learners, families, and communities: they have an in-depth knowledge of their learners as they exist in their school and community. He has experienced how different the context can be for learners as he changed jobs from one district to the next. The appropriate tactics to achieve the best learning outcomes for learners in one setting may not work in another setting. This brings Rob to the second part of the definition of "staying true to yourself." The learner, and the learning experience, must be the center of the entire learning ecosystem. The guiding principle of being learner-centered provides a focus for school leaders that allow them to adapt tactics appropriate for their context. For this reason, during the current crisis, staying true to learners must be the lens through which we navigate this crisis.

STAYING TRUE TO YOURSELF

Opening the door to the school and walking into the empty hallway, he notices Jane, the elementary principal, working in her office. Jane is an exceptional leader who learned long ago how to lead by staying focused on short and long-term goals for her learners and staff. Jane

> ## STAYING TRUE TO YOURSELF
>
> Staying true to yourself occurs when you know that your everyday actions and decisions further your dreams that you have for your learners, school, and community.

exemplifies Rob's vision of staying true to yourself: never forgetting why you became an educator in the first place.

One of Rob's "go-to" jokes is that he has never met a school leader who decided to be an educator because they wanted to administer standardized tests. Many times, after years of changes, educators forget their core beliefs and purpose for starting a career in education. Staying focused on your core beliefs and purposes is the most important job for a school leader. Too often, distractions caused by positional power, politics, or management steer school leaders away from their core beliefs and purpose. Jane does not allow distractions to detour her from staying true to herself and staying focused on why she chose to be an educator.

STAYING TRUE TO YOUR STAFF

> ### STAYING TRUE TO YOUR STAFF
>
> Staying true to your staff occurs when you use empathy to understand what your staff is experiencing now, what they will experience in the future and to empower them to grow professionally.

Rob has almost made his way back to his office. Along the way, he stopped and peered into a few classrooms. If he wasn't so excited about his revelation on the walking path, he might find himself getting melancholy looking at all those empty desks. However, because of his excitement, the quiet classrooms remind him of his third principle, staying true to your staff. This principle is straight forward. Without staff buy-in, no significant change will occur in your school. The work of ingraining a learner-centered mindset into the school structure requires everyone in the system to contribute. Every time he opens the door to his office, as he is doing now, Rob reminds himself that he can't do the work of incorporating a learner-centered focus into the school by himself. The school district administration cannot do the work themselves. Leadership comes from everywhere within the school district. Staying true to your staff involves three key facets:

1. Including your staff on all aspects of planning and implementation of an initiative.
2. Making sure the staff has the knowledge and skills necessary to make the changes you want to implement. Spend the time and money to make sure this happens.
3. Asking the staff what new knowledge and skills they think they need to implement the initiative.

Rob's not fond of "buzz words" in education. Jargon is the reason there's too much complexity in schools right now. However, the three critical facets of staying true to your staff are summed up in one word: empowerment. When the staff knows they are being treated as professionals,

> ## EMPOWERMENT
>
> Empowerment is a frequently used word in this book. Empowerment happens when staff or learners have meaningful input into decisions affecting them and are given authority to take independent action

and their input is meaningful, then they become ambassadors for the initiative the school is undertaking.

Rob remembers one of his core beliefs: teachers interacting with students is everything. Nothing comes before or gets in the way of that invaluable interaction. Everything else is secondary. Staying true to learners occurs when teachers are interacting with them. To help all staff with creating the conditions to create the best learning experiences, they must remember to stay true to themselves. When these three principles are working in unison, a school system can navigate its way through any crisis. As Rob walks through the doorway to his office, he is renewed and excited about the future of the school district...but still a bit nervous about pulling this off.

BOOK STUDY QUESTIONS FOR PROLOGUE

1. Currently, how do you stay true to learners in a crisis?
2. Currently, how do you stay true to yourself in a crisis?
3. Currently, how do you stay true to your staff in a crisis?
4. Think of times of significant disruption in your work life. What actions did you take to meet the challenges?

STAY TRUE TO YOUR LEARNERS

THE NEW LEARNING ECOSYSTEM

"Big thinking precedes great achievement."

—WILFERD PETERSON

CHAPTER 1 CONCEPTS AND THINK-ABOUTS

1. The difference between crisis management and crisis leadership
2. Why "adult convenience" keeps schools from innovating
3. The importance of empowering teachers
4. The New Learning Ecosystem
5. The three instructional models in The New Learning Ecosystem
6. The importance of virtualization of instruction, curriculum, and assessment in The New Learning Ecosystem

Rob enters his office, and he feels his heart thumping...as much from the excitement of his revelation on the path as the physical exertion of his walk. He quickly sits down at his desk and calls Jane. He knows that Jane is finishing up the lunch program for needy families and hopes she'll have a few minutes to talk.

"Hey Jane, do you have a minute to come to my office? I have an idea that I want to run by you?" Rob asks. Jane recognizes the familiar sense of urgency and excitement in Rob's voice and tells him she will be right over.

It seems like hours to Rob before Jane walks in the door, but in truth, only a few minutes passed before Jane peeked her head around the corner. "Ready for me, boss?" Jane asks with a smile.

"Come in, Jane, thank you for coming at such short notice. How is the lunch program going?"

Jane steps into Rob's office and takes a seat across from his desk. "Great! Today we packed over 700 lunches and sent them out on the busses for deliveries. I just feel so much better that our kids are getting these lunches from the school. It just shows our community how much we care."

RADICALLY LEARNER-CENTERED

Radically learner-centered focus occurs when all decisions within the school system are made through the lens of what is best for every individual learner. Decisions are not made for adult convenience.

"More than that," Rob chimes in, "It shows that we are living our value of being radically learner-centered. We are backing our words up with actions...making sure all our kids are fed. This is why I called you in. I want to talk about how our core value of being radically learner-centered is going to lead us through this COVID-19 crisis."

Jane smiles. She knows that Rob's bedrock conviction about school and kids is being radically learner-centered. Jane has participated in many discussions over the years with Rob about becoming radically learner-centered.

"Jane, this may seem weird, but I had a revelation when I went for a walk this morning. I stopped and listened to a red-winged blackbird. The song was so beautiful, and I became absorbed in it. I became so focused on that bird that all the problems we have been facing because of the pandemic were forgotten for a few moments. Suddenly, the path forward for our school district became clear to me," Rob began.

"We have focused all of our work since you and I started working together in this school district on making sure the learner is at the center of everything that we do...period...no questions asked. Would you agree, Jane?" Rob asked.

"Oh, absolutely," Jane jumps in excitedly. "I believe The New Learning Ecosystem diagram that we created has served as a foundation for making sure all students are at the center of every decision that we make. And boy, have some of those decisions been against the grain of what 'normal' school districts do!" She laughs.

"How about it," Rob grins as he remembers some of those decisions. "Our laser focus on the ecosystem has been our guiding light for everything that we do. The revelation that came to me on my walk is that now, more than ever, we have to double down on The New Learning Ecosystem as our North Star to make decisions during the crisis we're facing."

"I think a renewed focus will provide clarity and focus for our staff and the larger community," Jane responds. "I see a benefit for everyone in our school system to hear that our goals and vision for the school district have not changed despite the challenges we face right now. We are experiencing an unexpected detour in our journey, but the destination stays the same."

CRISIS MANAGEMENT VERSUS CRISIS LEADERSHIP

ROB SITS BACK in his chair and places his hands behind his head. He stares into space, and Jane wonders if he is staring at the wall or if he has created a vision of the future in his mind and is "living" in it right now. Probably the latter, if she knows Rob, she thinks.

Rob comes out of his trance and says, "Let's look at this time and place in the crisis and think of crisis management and crisis leadership. We experience crisis management when we make urgent decisions that determine the survival of the school district. We started in crisis management the second the Governor first shut down all the schools in the State. We had to figure out the mobile lunch program, personnel issues, internet connectivity issues of our staff and learners, and any number of other urgent items that needed immediate attention."

Rob leans forward with enthusiasm, "At the same time, we cannot become so engrossed in crisis management that we forget crisis leadership. In crisis leadership, we keep in mind the long-term goals of the district. More than just thinking about them, we leverage the current situation to help our school district reach the goals and vision we have already established. Dare I say we may even be able to reach the vision sooner because of the crisis? I have created a Venn diagram explaining the relationship between crisis management and crisis leadership."

Rob shuffles through some papers on his desk and finds the diagram. He passes it to Jane so she can have a look at it.

Jane takes the piece of paper with the diagram on it and looks it over. "Rob, what you are asking leaders in the school district to do is to shift our leadership mindset. During the first few months of the crisis, we have focused so much on the short-term activities that we may have neglected thinking about our long-term ambitions for our school, our students, our staff, and ourselves. I don't think we have done anything wrong by having a short-term focus because we needed to have that focus during the initial crisis. This is management. What I hear you say is that we now must be reflective and make sure long-term thinking, otherwise known as crisis leadership, is on our leadership radar screens."

"You've hit the nail on the head, Jane," answers Rob. "Now is not the time to slow down or allow fear to overcome us. We have to keep moving forward with a singular focus on creating the future we developed with all of the stakeholders in the school district."

"Do you remember the school board meeting three years ago when we introduced the idea of The New Learning Ecosystem to the school board?" Rob asks. "I sure do," Jane replies. "Boy, was everyone nervous. We worked hard as a leadership team to

> ## THE NEW LEARNING ECOSYSTEM
>
> A framework of learning that places the learner and the learning experience at the center of all decisions.

come up with a great concept, but we were apprehensive about how the idea would work with the school board."

"I remember the feeling of apprehension as well," he answers. Just the thought of that night's board meeting causes him to get up from his chair and pace around his office.

Rob continues talking while he grabs a dry erase marker and starts sketching The New Learning Ecosystem on the whiteboard in his office. "I remember your responsibility that night was to convey a sense of urgency for why The New Learning Ecosystem was needed. You had to explain to the school Board why they needed to think differently about how education and schooling worked. I can still remember your opening statement to the Board. You did such a great job creating a framework for the Board, so they had context for the rest of the presentation."

Jane chuckles at the memory of that night. "What's funny, Rob, is that I have discussed The New Learning Ecosystem and the sense of urgency required to make it happen so many times since then to community groups and staff that I sometimes wake up in the middle of the night dreaming about it!"

Rob laughs. "I don't know if that says something about your dedication to your job or your lack of a social life! But seriously, I know what you mean. The amount of work it took to communicate our vision for the school district became all-encompassing. Do you remember your voice cracking with nerves when you introduced the presentation?"

"Yes, I do! I remember looking up to see you smiling. That gesture put me at ease and made the rest of the presentation go much smoother for me. By the way," Jane continues, "I see where you are starting to sketch The New Learning Ecosystem on the whiteboard. It is worth noting that the school board, the school district, the leadership team, staff, and community have not wavered from our belief that The New Learning Ecosystem is the best thing for our kids."

ADULT CONVENIENCE AND COMMAND AND CONTROL

ROB STOPS WRITING on the whiteboard and steps back to look at it. The crux of The New Learning Ecosystem is shifting the focus away from adult convenience and toward being learner-centered. Rob recalls Jane's presentation that night three years ago at the school board meeting and how well she made that point to the Board.

Jane first introduced the problem of adult convenience and command and control. "The current learning ecosystem places adult convenience at the center, or starting point, of all education decisions," she began. "Let's consider what 'adult convenience' means. We have grades to compare and sort the learners. We have buildings so we can control the learners. We create schedules centered on where the adults need to be during the day, not where the learners will be in their learning. We have rooms where all learning is supposed to take place. We have courses where learners are exposed to information in a regimented fashion. Learners move through the system in batches (or grade levels) based on their date of birth. The result is that our current industrial age learning ecosystem is a command and control organizational model. The learners contribute to the ecosystem, but they are not the total focus of the system. Other considerations become more critical, and the bureaucracy drives the system, not the learner."

Rob is now drawing a circle on his whiteboard as he and Jane recount the events from the board meeting. Rob is putting the finishing touches on a diagram that he and the school's leadership team has used many times to visualize the problem of adult convenience and command and control.

"That diagram reminds me of what you told the board when you so rudely interrupted me during my presentation," says Jane, with a raised eyebrow and a smile.

"I know, I know, I just couldn't help myself, "Rob answers. "I hope you didn't take my breaking in like that to be rude."

Jane shakes her head and says, "Not at all. The story you told fit in perfectly with the point I was trying to make. I can still remember what you said."

"Me, too. I recall the story well. It's my 'master schedule' story." Rob finishes writing "master schedules" on his diagram on the whiteboard.

I told the Board, 'I bet some of you are saying, 'Of course we make all decisions based on what is best for our kids...how dare you say different!' My answer to that question is this... 'Have you ever made a master schedule for a school?' I made many master schedules during my time as a guidance counselor and principal. Although I enjoyed the challenge of putting all the puzzle pieces together to make the schedule work, the task was not learner-centered. As a matter of fact, it may have been the most adult-oriented thing I did as an educator. After all, the entire point of a master schedule is to place students in boxes dictated by the necessities and desires of adults.'"

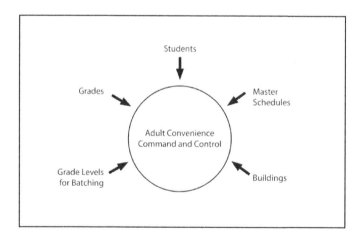

Jane stands up from the chair, takes a marker, and circles "master schedule." "The story you shared with the Board in a lot of ways is the crux of the problem with adult convenience and command and control in the school system. When that is the lens in which schools make decisions, the true needs of the students get so warped that they are forgotten."

"After your story, I remember taking the temperature of the room. I wanted to see how the school board reacted to your story since shining a spotlight on adult convenience in our school system challenges people's ideas about the purpose of school. I remember thinking, 'So far, so good. No one is checking their cell phones yet'."

Rob erases the words "command and control" in the diagram and rewrites them with a red marker. "I just rewrote this in red because command and control manifests itself in an outdated school system in diabolical ways. It is more than just a boss, or a teacher, telling someone what to do. It's how control ingrains itself in the way everyone within the school thinks. Simple things like having classroom chairs in nice, tidy rows is an example of a control mentality. I remember all of us worrying about how Gene would react to this."

Gene was the board member with a military background and the one Board member in which the leadership identified as the one who might rebel most against the idea that 'command and control' is a problem.

Jane takes the red marker from Rob and draws a circle around the words "command and control" and draws a line diagonal across the circle a la Ghostbusters. "I looked up that night at the meeting and saw Gene nodding his head in agreement with your story, and I knew that we were doing well."

"But we weren't out of the woods yet," Rob answers as he steps away from the whiteboard to look at his handiwork from a different angle. "What you were saying next in the presentation pushed Gene and the rest of the board even further."

"Yes, I told them that a school system based on command and control has never worked well for all learners. Some learners could game the system by 'playing school' ...figuring out the 'right' answers or doing just enough to get by. This often meant being compliant and not getting into trouble," Jane replies. "That's the problem with the old way and why The New Learning Ecosystem is so important. Playing school by being compliant is not suitable for individual learners. All learners need to be engaged."

"Jane, let's look hard at The New Learning Ecosystem that I have sketched on the whiteboard," Rob suggests as he moves a chair from the corner of the room to in front of the whiteboard. "What is the one thing you wished you would have known the night of the presentation to the Board that you know now? What have you learned because you have presented it to so many community groups over the past three years?"

Jane approaches the whiteboard again. Rob thinks she is going to take a marker and start to write something, but instead, she points her finger at the center of The New Learning Ecosystem.

"If I had to do over again'" Jane begins, "I would have said more about why the current system of adult convenience came to dominate the world of education. There were always students that did not engage in the old ecosystem of education. Learners not engaging with their schoolwork was never good, but in the 20TH

> ## MY TWO CENTS
>
> Disengaged students no longer have the luxury of well-paying jobs waiting for them when they leave our system disengaged. Well paying, life-affirming jobs simply are not readily available for our disengaged learners

Century—during peak industrialization—it was tolerated by the adults because the disengaged learners could still become productive members of society as they moved to jobs in the industrial economy. Today, disengaged students no longer have the luxury of well-paying jobs waiting for them when they leave our system. Well paying, life-affirming jobs simply are not readily available for our disengaged learners."

"That fits in perfectly with the message we wanted the Board to walk away with that night," Rob explains. The bottom line is that schools can no longer exist for adult convenience. Instead, we must change our learning ecosystem to be radically learner-centered. Radically learner-centered means that the entire structure and system of schooling and education revolves around learners and the things they need to be successful. All decisions must be made with the learner being at the center of decision making. That is the crux of The New Learning Ecosystem."

Turning around to face Rob, Jane looks pensive. "I can remember my heart jumping into my throat when Jeanie's hand went up to ask a question. You and I both know that Jeanie uses the ties that she built as a teacher in the district to disrupt ideas we bring to the Board that she does not like. Jeanie is always trying to protect the old way of doing things."

Rob remembers being very apprehensive when he saw Jeanie's hand go up. "I sure was relieved when Jeanie looked you in the eye and said, 'I agree with what you are saying about the changes that have occurred in our society where kids can't just go out and get good, middle-class jobs without a good education. I never looked at it from the point of view of 'command and control,' but I can see where it is a problem. I just hope that I will hear how we will also preserve the best of what we do now in school and change only what we need to change.'"

Jane and Rob look up at the same time and see Craig in the doorway. Craig is the high school principal. Jane and Craig worked together when she was an assistant principal at the high school. Rob knows first-hand how passionate Craig is about keeping the best interests of the kids at the forefront of everything the school does. Of all the principals in the school district, Craig may have the most "learner-centered" philosophy of anyone. That's not to say he is a pushover and lets learners walk over him—far from it. Rob has seen the courage Craig exhibits to "live his values" while making decisions based on what is best for learners.

"Come on in, Craig!" Rob invites Craig into the office by sliding a chair to the front of the whiteboard. "As you can see, Jane and I are talking about The New Learning Ecosystem for the millionth time! In all seriousness, I think our focus on The New Learning Ecosystem is more important now during the pandemic than at any other time in my career. I was sharing with Jane how I believe it will be the foundational piece that helps our school district navigate the pandemic. We were just reliving the night three years ago when the leadership team presented the concept of The New Learning Ecosystem to the school board."

"Let's not throw the baby out with the bathwater," Craig says as he walks into the office toward the empty chair Rob has made available for him.

Both Rob and Jane look at Craig quizzically and ask at the same time, "What?"

"Remember, that was my little contribution to that night. While the leadership team was preparing the presentation, I kept saying that we cannot give the impression that we want to end everything they know and understand about education. As a leadership team, we believe we can shift to The New Learning Ecosystem while keeping the best parts of the old ecosystem. In other words, we don't want to throw the baby out with the bathwater."

"Ah, yes, I do remember that now!" Rob answers. "By saying that, you helped the school board, and the townsfolk, feel more comfortable with the changes we were asking them to make to the system of education— that even though what we were asking of them was a radical change, that they could still use what worked well for them as long as it was learner-centered."

"Jane, do you remember what you said to me as I took my turn at the podium that night?" Craig asks her.

Jane smiles and nods at Craig. "Of course, I remember. I told you that you were going to be great during your part of the presentation and to remember to speak through your soul."

Rob knows that Craig reacts best when he declutters his mind and connects with his passion for kids. Out of all of the school leaders in the school district, Rob knows Craig responds the best to his personal, elemental reason for becoming an educator: to help all kids.

"I was also looking for the start of flop sweat on you but didn't see any!" Jane kids Craig. Jane excuses herself from the room and informs Rob and Craig that she will be back shortly.

Rob walks behind his desk and grabs for a book on his bookshelf. He pulls out the book Inevitable: Mass Customized Learning: Learning in the Age of Empowerment by Chuck Schwahn and Bea McGarvey.

"This is the book that started our journey. Do you remember reading it for the first time, Craig?" Rob asks.

"I sure do," Craig answers as he takes the book from Rob and looks through the highlights and dog-eared pages. "Our idea of The New Learning Ecosystem has its roots in this book."

Rob sits back down behind his desk. "I thought your explanation to the school board at our meeting three years ago was the part that sealed the deal with them."

"What I said back then is as true today as it was back then," Craig begins, "A new ecosystem is needed to empower learners and the professionals that lead schools. The current education reforms, and reformers consistently

> ## MY TWO CENTS
>
> The current education reforms - and reformers - consistently underestimate learners and educators.

underestimate learners and educators. The key to a significant change in our system lies within these two groups. Empowering the learners to craft their learning experiences, with help from an adult, creates a system that places the learner at the center of The New Learning Ecosystem. Stripping away the barriers of the old learning ecosystem allows educators to flourish in a setting where their experiences and expertise can directly benefit learners."

Three years ago, the leadership team paid close attention to the Board to gauge their reaction to what Craig was telling them. One of the underlying issues in the community was the teacher strike that happened 25 years ago. The leadership team hoped that the scars from that bad time in the district had passed, but Rob reminded the leadership team to be aware that it could still rear its ugly head. The key to the success of the New Learning Ecosystem is the staff and teachers. They hold the key to the success or failure of the idea by how well they engage and believe in The New Learning Ecosystem.

Craig continues, "Any ecosystem is a dynamic force where various parts give and take energy from each other to create a balance and make the entire system work. Our current education ecosystem is dangerously out of balance. Education happens to the learners, not with them. Remember the old ecosystem where learners contribute to the system and are not the sole purpose for the system? There is minimal opportunity for meaningful input by learners into the old ecosystem. Everything within the old system is coming at them, not being created by them and that's the critical difference."

Rob leans forward in his chair as he interrupts Craig, "The same dynamic holds for the educators in the old, industrialized system. Their role in the ecosystem is to absorb, not to contribute. In truth, the old education ecosystem has turned into a black hole. Any educational change that comes into the gravitational pull of the old educational system is distorted as it is pulled toward adult convenience. Lost in this milieu of policies, reforms, and programs is the real purpose of education: to assure the learner is learning. Learner and teacher empowerment is baked into the DNA of The New Learning Ecosystem."

Jane walks back into the office. She is holding a platter of fruit. "I ordered this for our faculty meeting today, and these are the leftovers. The sugar will help us stay focused!" She puts the platter down on Rob's desk. "I also remember when we said the DNA of The New Learning Ecosystem consisted of the learner and teacher empowerment. Empowerment of the staff and students is the fuel that runs The New Learning Ecosystem engine. I recall the entire Board nodded their heads in agreement—what a relief that was! Even Freddy, the one Board member who tends to doze during presentations, stayed awake."

Rob and Craig get up from their chairs, both grab a napkin and take some fruit. "Thank you for getting this for us," Rob says as he takes a bite of watermelon. "We're going to need the sustenance to keep us going until we have a plan of action!"

TEACHER EMPOWERMENT

ROB SITS BACK down in his chair and starts to talk about how he became a proponent of teacher empowerment. "I always enjoy my time when I go out and walk through classes and meet the learners and the teachers. One time when I was walking through one of the elementary schools, I heard teachers in similar grade levels teaching exactly the same lesson at the same time, right down to echoing the same instructions to the learners. When I asked Karen—a principal at another elementary school in the school district—about this, she told me the entire district made sure all of the grade level teachers were teaching the same thing on the same day in every classroom. This was done to ensure the reading and math programs were implemented with 'fidelity.' I was aghast. 'implementing with fidelity' to me means de-professionalizing teachers and not allowing them to use their experience and expertise to know when to introduce topics to their students. We don't allow that practice in The New Learning Ecosystem, and we have to stay true to that mission during our current crisis—even when COVID-19 makes us want to return to what's 'comfortable.'"

All three look up at the sound of footsteps and see Karen walking into the office. Karen is the most experienced of the district leadership team. She spent over 20 years in the classroom before becoming an administrator. For this reason, teachers in the district respect her and follow her lead because they know she has "been there" with them. Karen is a natural performer in front of any group. Rob jokes that she is the Pied Piper of the school district because when she explains what she wants to do, people will follow her to get it done.

THE NEW LEARNING ECOSYSTEM

KAREN LOOKS AT The New Learning Ecosystem that is drawn on the whiteboard and says, "What's going on here?"

Rob stands up and offers Karen his seat while Craig goes into the lobby to grab another chair.

Rob explains, "I started this conversation with Jane earlier to share a thought that I had about how to navigate the COVID-19 crisis. To make a long story short, I think we need to double down on our original vision of The New Learning Ecosystem. We can't change or veer off course because of the crisis. I know that everything is topsy-turvy right now in the education world, but we have to stay grounded in The New Learning Ecosystem."

THE NEW LEARNING ECOSYSTEM

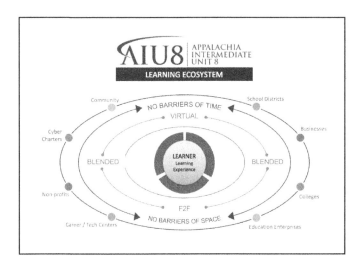

"I agree with you, Rob," Karen says. "I love The New Learning Ecosystem because at the heart of the ecosystem is the learner and the learning experience. Creating learning experiences for the learner that are relevant, engaging, and meet the learning needs of the learner may seem obvious. Still, it does not happen in enough old education ecosystem. The very fact of the matter is that placing the learner and the learning experience at the center of everything the school does is actually radical."

When the team was creating the presentation for the school board, they were leery about using the word "radical." Some of the most pointed conversations among the leadership team centered on this one word. Would it scare people off? Is it too political? What does it even mean in today's society? After trying to come up with other words, the team just kept coming back to the word "radical." To them, it had no political overtones. It sent a powerful message that things must change in the way schools operate.

Rob remembers looking around the room and checking the reactions of the school board members. Gene fidgeted a little bit, and there may be a slight frown on Jeanie's face, but things looked good.

Getting fired up, Karen continues "When filtering all decisions based on the learner being at the center, barriers of growth and opportunity for the student fall by the wayside. The learner and the learning experience become the focal point, not the adult convenience that governs the old ecosystem. All decisions by the school board, administration, and teachers are filtered through the lens of being radically learner-centered.

Placing the Learner at the center of the ecosystem is a radical act. When we believe that each individual learner deserves their most optimal learning experience, the realm of possibilities for the learner expand. No longer will we accept that a learner cannot take a 'course' because it will not fit into their schedule. Additionally, those valuable learning experiences that are community-based will not be saved just for a few learners doing an internship: they will be available for all learners.

Learners will no longer be held hostage to time. Their learning experiences are created so they can engage with the content when they are ready for it, on their own terms. Time will be a variable that adjusts to the needs of each individual learner. Placing the learner at the center shows the old industrial model of schooling for what it is...a fraud." Karen pauses to take a bite of kiwi fruit as Jane and Craig nod with enthusiasm.

Even today, three years after the presentation and amidst a pandemic, Rob gets somewhat nervous about trashing the old education ecosystem. The industrial economy worked well for his family. It created the conditions that allowed him and his brothers and sisters to go to college and to live the American dream. Trashing the industrial model is fraught with challenges, but ultimately, the industrial model is not a good fit for the society and job market that we have today.

Rob walks over to the whiteboard and points to the drawing of The New Learning Ecosystem. "The best way to guarantee that learners are placed at the center of the ecosystem is to empower teachers to accomplish the task. The teaching profession has been inundated with reforms that degrade the professionalism of teachers while at the same time punishing them for instituting reform measures that simply make no sense. People say: 'show me the proof that The New Learning Ecosystem will work.' I always ask them a question in return, 'Show me any proof that what we are doing now in education is doing right for all learners.'" Rob was now getting passionate.

"Empowering teachers to use their professional knowledge and experience to create learning experiences for learners seems to be a common-sense place to start. After all, who interacts with the learners more than the teachers? Teachers, rightfully so, have become cynical to changes in the education field as they have seen reforms come and go throughout their careers.

How many times have teachers been tasked with placing the learner and the learning experience at the center of everything that happens in the school? Not many times, if at all. Once teachers have faith that their professional judgment matters and that the industrial-age structure, which limits their participation in the educational system, is disintegrating, they will create the best learning experiences for learners." Rob finishes, takes a few steps back and asks Karen a question.

THE LEARNING EXPERIENCE

"KAREN, SOMETHING THAT has changed in our thinking since we presented The New Learning Ecosystem three years ago is the importance of the learning experience. You and I have talked about it quite a bit, but do you mind sharing our thoughts with Jane and Craig, as well?"

"Sure, Rob," Karen answers as she grabs a marker and begins drawing on the whiteboard.

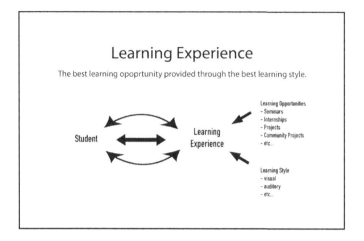

"The heart of making the entire learning ecosystem radically learner-centered is the learning experience," Karen begins. "The definition of a learning experience, when viewed through the lens of a learner, is 'The best learn-

> ## THE LEARNING EXPERIENCE
>
> The best learning opportunity provided through the best learning style.

ing opportunity provided through the best learning style.' Creating a learning experience is not a simple, cut and dried formula where a teacher can plug data into an algorithm, and out comes a learning experience. During the creation of a learning experience, we must consider two things: learning opportunities and learning styles. Learning opportunities are what teachers can use to help the learner interact with new content. They can be projects, internships, seminars, community projects, or regular instruction delivered virtually or face to face. Most schools stop at the learning opportunity stage because they are not as learner-focused as we are. We take the creation of the learning experience further by seriously considering the learning style of all of our kids and what works best for them as individuals."

Rob knows the idea of learning styles is somewhat controversial both with community members and among staff. Many people in the community hold the belief that "what was good enough for me when I was in school is good enough for the kids today" attitude. Rob has heard a variation of this comment many times as he's talked about The New Learning Ecosystem with members of the school community. He has also had many conversations with his staff about this topic. Some of the staff mistakenly believe that matching learning styles means "differentiated learning." Differentiated learning is a great attempt at creating personalized learning experiences...but it is doomed to fail. If a teacher has a class with 25 learners in it, crafting a lesson unique to each student is simply not sustainable.

Karen finishes the drawing on the whiteboard and turns around to face the group. "What is important about The New Learning Ecosystem and creating great learning experiences is that we are questioning the old way of doing things. More than questioning, we want to embed a new mindset in our schools that allow our teachers to work effectively with all our learners. As a quick example, are there better ways of grouping learners during their school day? Traditionally, schools group learners by grade level, then by subject, then by grades. We don't want to do that anymore. It's not effective. In the best of all possible worlds, grouping learners by taking our curriculum and creating learning progression that allows learners to move through the progressions at their own pace with other similar learners seems more appropriate."

THE LEARNING EXPERIENCE PLATFORM

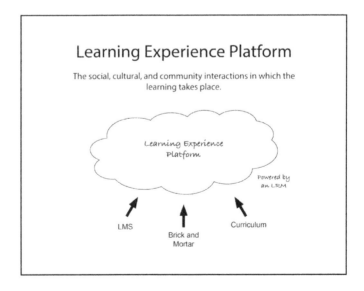

"Thank you, Karen," Jane holds her hand out for the marker from Karen and walks to the whiteboard.

"Karen's comments get to the heart of what Rob and I are calling the 'Learning Experience Platform.' As a leadership team, we have thought deeply about how to look at learning experiences through the eyes of our learners. We even included learners in our discussion—after all, who better to ask?"

Jane finishes her graphic on the whiteboard. "As you can see on the Board, we have defined the Learning Experience Platform as the social, cultural, and community interactions in which learning takes place. Learning occurs through a curriculum, traditional

> ## THE LEARNING EXPERIENCE PLATFORM
>
> Learning Experience Platform is the social, cultural, and community interactions in which learning takes place.

learning environments (school buildings, internships, mentorships, etc.), and a learning management system that helps students and staff manage all the learning experiences. Simply put, the Learning Experience Platform is a place where the learning experiences of the learner are managed. Something that came up repeatedly in our conversations with learners, their parents, and teachers was that to have one place where they could log into and see all of their learning and their options is essential."

Rob gazes out of his office window at the empty recreational fields as Jane leads the discussion about the Learning Experience Platform. He finds himself thinking back to the night of the Board meeting when Jane was explaining the idea of a learning experience platform. He cringes a little bit at the memory. Two of the more vocal Board members spoke up to ask questions. Rob can still remember the exchange between Jane and the Board.

"Wait a minute," Gene broke in. "You are throwing a lot of education mumbo-jumbo out there. What the heck is an LMS? Better yet, why should I care about it?"

"Sorry about that, Gene" Jane responded to Gene with a sincere smile on her face. "I know educators can get a little carried away at times with our jargon and our acronyms. 'LMS' stands for 'learning management system.' Think of an LMS as a classroom where learners go online to get their instruction when they are learning online. For example, a learner might have six different classes during their school day, and in the LMS they could 'see' all of their classes. A learner can see their assignments, grades, messages from their teacher, resources for their class, and even videos and audio resources. If a teacher uses a resource that is not internal to the LMS, the students still know where to go to find the link to that resource. An LMS prevents learners and their families from having to log-in to multiple, separate resources. It is also important to remember that using an LMS does not mean a school or a classroom is an 'online school.' An LMS is a place where learners and teachers can go to interact and share resources, whether they are in a traditional brick and mortar setting, or an online environment. Does that answer your question, Gene?"

Jeanie piped up, "When I was a teacher, I always made sure all of my students were given instruction that was tailored to their specific needs."

Jane worked with Jeanie for 15 years and knows that she did not, in fact, tailor her lessons all the time to meet the needs of every learner. This meeting was not the time or setting to argue that point, though.

"It wasn't that long ago that we worked together, Jeanie," Jane begins her response. "I know you remember how hard we had to work even to try to create the best learning experiences for our learners. A lot of times, we were hampered by some of the structures of schooling that we couldn't change. Grades levels are an example. Imagine what you could have done if we could have grouped kids by where they are in the curriculum and not strictly by grade level; we both experienced kids that could move through the curriculum quicker than their classmates or needed more time to learn the curriculum. Cross-grade level grouping would have been a blessing back in those days!"

"You're right, Jane," Jeanie answers. "It was tough doing it the old fashion way."

"Thank you for using the words 'old fashioned way'," Jane replies. "Our goal of introducing the Learning Experience Platform is to give a framework to make the learning experience live in the real world. After all, a theory is great and may look good on paper, but our job in education is to make sure we can make the theory come alive for our learners. By the way, it's more than a job. It's our ethical responsibility to do what is right for learners in every step of their education journey."

Rob is brought back to the present day when Natalie walks into his office. What began as a discussion with Jane about how the school district's vision will get them through the pandemic has turned into an impromptu leadership team meeting. Natalie tells the group that she has been eavesdropping on the conversation for a few minutes while she waited for some paperwork from the HR office.

Natalie sits in the chair that Rob offers her and says, "I want to speak from my heart. When we talk about 'learning experiences' and learning experience platforms' we cannot forget that we are talking about real, honest to goodness kids. One aspect of our current education structure is an unhealthy reliance on testing data.

> ## QUOTE
>
> End of year testing, and the data is produces, has not been good for kids. It may be good for some people working in education think tanks, but this reliance on testing data, we believe, has been detrimental for our learners.

End of year testing and the data it produces has not been good for kids. It may be useful for some people working in education think tanks, but this reliance on testing data, I believe, has been detrimental for our learners."

Natalie sees that she has the attention of her colleagues. She walks up to the whiteboard and forcefully places her finger at the center of The New Learning Ecosystem. Everyone present can hear the passion in her voice. "I do not want my children, or ANY CHILD, to simply be a test score. I want my children and ALL CHILDREN, to be wrapped in a system of support and caring that supports intellectual and emotional development. I do not want my children, or ANY CHILD, to be in their 'zone of proximal development' based on where a test score slots them into. I want my children and ALL CHILDREN to have learning experiences that are customized to their entire being. I do not want my children, or ANY CHILD, to be in the red, green, or yellow 'zone of growth' in a 'growth model.' I want my children, and ALL CHILDREN, to learn the power of creativity and harness their imagination for lifelong learning. I do not want my children, or ANY CHILD, to be labeled as 'in need of support' because they did not do well on a meaningless State-mandated test. I want my children, and ALL CHILDREN, to learn from their mistakes and use critical thinking to make decisions."

The room is still. Rob thinks it's a good time to close the circle on the conversation and come back to their present predicament. "Thank you, Natalie, for speaking from your heart. In the coming weeks and months, it will be so important for all of us to lead with our hearts. The rules of the 'education game' are going to change on a weekly, or even daily basis as our lawmakers try to adapt to the pandemic. Our job is to remain focused on the kids, stay calm, and lead with integrity and purpose."

Rob can feel the positive energy buzzing in the room. He walks around Jane and Craig to get back to his desk. "We have spent a lot of time talking to the Board, our parents, community, and learners about what learning is. Our definition of learning does not include something memorized by a learner for a short time, so they get a good grade on a test. We want to see evidence that learners understand a concept that is unique and transferable to other contexts. Admittedly, this is a high bar, but one we feel is achievable. The State-mandated tests will not give us this kind of information. Second, we want learners to try to do well on the tests, but we also are frank with them about our motivation for them to do well. We believe that preparing and trying your best is what is important and not the actual result. Theoretically, if the school has done our job, the results of these tests should be good. We believe the New Learning Ecosystem, operationalized by learning experiences and the learning experience platform, places learning at the forefront, not a test score."

Rob's office is large, but not large enough to comfortably fit all the people that are now in it. Jane suggests that the meeting be moved to the conference room down the hall where there's more space. Everyone agrees that this is a good idea. The group files down the hallway to the conference room and passes Brett's office. Brett is the business manager and an integral part of the leadership team.

"Why don't you join us for a few minutes?" Rob asks as he walks by the office. "We are having a great discussion about what our mindset should be to best navigate the COVID-19 pandemic and your input would be valuable."

Brett stands from his chair and walks toward the door and says,

"Sounds like a plan. I just finished running the numbers for our Title I budget, so I need a little bit of a break."

Brett had helped the district through a lot of financial storms, so he had a lot of clout with the school board and the business community. Even the most disagreeable Board member would trust Brett's recommendations to the Board.

THE OLD STRUCTURE OF SCHOOL

AS THE TEAM settles around the conference table, Rob opens the refrigerator, grabs some water bottles, and passes them out to the team. As he is passing out the water, he asks Brett to share his thoughts on the old structure of schooling. Rob has been helping Brett with a paper for an organizational development class for his MBA and knows this has been a focus for Brett's work.

Brett agrees and begins, "The managerial structure of the old educational ecosystem was based on the industrial model of production and in an image of a factory. When the high school model was created at the turn of the 20TH Century, industrialists like Henry Ford and Andrew Carnegie were creating massive factories that regimented the manufacturing process for better efficiencies. Taking their cue from industry, education leaders copied

> ### MY TWO CENTS
>
> The history of the schooling model is essential for school leaders to understand. The saying "form follows function" holds true in this case. The model of schooling was adopted from the industrialists and meant to mimic the structure of a factory. When we understand this history, we can better adjust our thinking and change our structures to meet the needs of the learners and our communities.

the factory model when creating the modern American school. What this meant in industry was the workers, especially in the Ford plants, had to do small tasks repeatedly. They were not allowed to vary from the prescribed routine; if they did, the entire manufacturing process would break down. To assure the workers did exactly what they were told, a management structure was created for control of the factories."

This leads to a discussion amongst the leadership team about the management structure of the current education system. As the conversation progresses, everyone realizes that this topic was not one that educational leadership programs at universities spent a lot of time covering. The management structure in education has been adopted and just assumed to be the only way to manage public education. Sure, there have been attempts to do something different (tinkering around the edges with things like "school-based budgeting"), but nothing that really addresses how to change the underlying industrial-based, managerial structure. Rob strongly feels that to change the management structure, you must change the learning structure for the kids. Form follows function.

Brett continues, "There were foremen on the factory floor to make sure the workers on the assembly line did their job. In turn, the foremen were overseen by supervisors to ensure they did their job exactly as prescribed. Supervisors were managed by factory superintendents and so on all the way up to the leader of the company. This command and control structure occurred in a specific space, in this case, the factory, to assure compliance toward company directives."

Rob now interjects as he leans back in his chair. "In the education world, the same structure from the factory was put in place and is still in place. Teachers are overseen by assistant principals, who are overseen by principals, who are managed by assistant superintendents or superintendents who are overseen by the school board. The entire structure of management that rules the school system is based on the premise that students and adults coexist in an educational factory. In factories, processes for work are streamlined to make the work 'idiot-proof.' In education—because we force people to come to one building to learn—policymakers have created curriculums that are scripted and, forgive me, 'idiot-proof.'. Oftentimes, the teacher reads from a prepared script to their students so that the 'bosses' in the system can be assured that the teaching process, not the learning process, is instituted the way deemed best by outside experts. The former example dehumanizes the factory worker, and the latter example de-professionalizes the teacher."

Rob is on a roll and there is no stopping him now.

"The other day, I was outside our high school at 3:00. The day was beautiful, with sunshine brightening the entire grounds of the school. We know that our school is newer with all of the latest educational 'gadgets' inside to help facilitate teaching. You all know where the student parking lot is and how you can see the entire width of the school with exits in the center and far left and far right. At 3:00, the bell rang. Within a minute, learners started to stream out the door toward the student parking lot and the busses. From my left streamed out the teachers with lunch bags and books tucked under each arm, heading to their parking lot. Within ten minutes, the building was mostly empty. I imagined that a factory at a shift change or quitting time would not have looked much different from the scene I witnessed at our school—all for the sake of perceived productivity and efficiency."

When the leadership team presented The New Learning Ecosystem to the school board, they realized that they had to offer a strong positive vision. Talking about what is wrong with the current system of education is a small part of building a positive vision of the future. The most difficult challenge is to craft a vision for the future that is easy to understand. The person on the leadership team that is perfect for the job is Diane. Diane has been working in the school district for 18 years. Her gift is explaining complex ideas in a way that everyone can understand. Diane is currently one of the middle school principals. She is always professional, punctual, and prepared. Rob had his secretary call her office and ask her to join the rest of the leadership team in the conference room and he briefs Diane on what he and the team have been discussing.

THE THREE INSTRUCTIONAL MODELS IN THE NEW LEARNING ECOSYSTEM

DIANE WALKS TO the whiteboard at the front of the conference room and sketches out a quick version of The New learning Ecosystem. She begins, "All of us here in this room know that the learner and the learning experience serves as the focus of the entire learning ecosystem. This fact implicitly suggests that the delivery model of learning is multi-faceted. The learner receives their learning in three ways. First, and most familiar to people, is face to face learning. Face to face learning is what occurs in school systems in the old educational ecosystem...and there is still a place for this type of learning in The New Learning Ecosystem. Learners sitting down with their peers and a teacher is a familiar model and valid when done in moderation. It is important that we do not 'throw the baby out with the bathwater,' as Craig likes to say, and jettison this traditional method of learning simply because it is associated with an outdated model that is bad for learners. We must recognize that face-to-face learning is an important—and viable—learning method. The New Learning Ecosystem simply implies that it is not the only learning method, and it should be done only after careful consideration."

Rob looks around the table as Diane is speaking. Everyone in the conference room has given a version of this talk to community service groups, parent organizations, and staff members. As Rob thinks about how to manage the school district during this current crisis effectively, he realizes the three instructional models are more important than ever. All three models will have to be used to deliver instruction to all their students effectively.

Diane is pacing in front of the conference room and Rob realizes she is suddenly coming to the same conclusion about the importance of the instructional models.

2 METHODS OF ONLINE INSTRUCTION

There are two methods of online instruction.

Synchronous is when learners meet "live" online with other learners and the teacher

Asynchronous is when learning material is made available for a learner and they progress through it at their own pace without meeting in a live session.

Diane continues, "A learning modality that is the polar opposite of face to face learning is where 100% of learner's instruction occurs in a virtual format. This is sometimes called 'online learning' or 'virtual learning.' In this model, the learners engage in learning experiences that are created and executed online. The learning experiences can range from ones in which the learners complete the experience entirely on their own without interaction with adults and other learners, to a model in which they interact with their teachers and other learners through virtual meetings. A common mistake that people make when they hear 'online learning' is that that they think it must mean a learner is plugged into a computer 100% of the time. Pictures of learners staring into computers in a huge classroom with no adult supervision come to mind for naysayers."

The leadership team consciously discussed these "worst-case scenarios" when they gave their public presentations. Addressing the worst-case scenario about virtual learning allows the team to build an alternate version of the possibilities of online education for people.

Diane continues, "Human nature will often take us to the worst-case scenario when considering a change from what we are used to doing. Any model that challenges the traditional face-to-face model of learning will bring out dystopian fears of learners staring at a computer screen all day long, not being engaged in their learning. We know that moderation in anything is important. Just like we know now that 100% face-to-face instruction is not optimal, 100% virtual instruction is not optimal. A virtual environment may work for some learners, but the reality is that most learners will not thrive in this system all the time. The New Learning Ecosystem suggests that learners receive some instruction in this format. The amount of time a learner spends in this modality will depend on their learning styles, goals for their learning, how their learning experiences are crafted, and the resources available within the larger school community."

Diane asks Rob to go to the whiteboard and circle the words "blended learning" in The New Learning Ecosystem. As he finishes his task, Diane wraps up her thoughts on the instructional models of The New Learning Ecosystem.

"The happy medium between 100% face-to-face and 100% online learning is called blended learning or hybrid learning. Blended learning is the sweet spot in The New Learning Ecosystem, where a learner receives their learning experience in the appropriate learning style based on their learning objectives. Blended learning allows teachers to create learning experiences that expand the reach of the typical classroom. Using a blended approach, teachers can access the truly outstanding learning experiences created throughout their community and the world. By incorporating blended learning models, teachers start to transition from being a teacher who transmits information to students, as they did in the outdated education structure, to a facilitator of learning as the learner and their learning experience take center stage."

VIRTUALIZATION OF INSTRUCTION, CURRICULUM, AND ASSESSMENT

ROB SMILES AS he thinks back to the school board meeting that started their journey to become radically learner-centered. He remembers looking around the board room as Diane explained these instructional models to them. He recalled that Gene hadn't looked down to count the food stains on his shirt yet (a sure sign that he is bored), Freddy hadn't fallen asleep, and Jeanie hadn't played "devil's advocate" (that's her favorite way to slow down a discussion she doesn't think is going in the direction she wants). A good meeting indeed!

VIRTUALIZATION OF INSTRUCTION

Virtualization of instruction involves two aspects.

Design of blended / online instruction:

Learn how to find, select and/or create quality content for the virtual environment (blended or online). This includes how to pull these resources together, pair them with a variety of online assessment strategies to craft meaningful learning experiences based on an understanding how people learn (design principles, multimedia use, layout, sequencing, sparking curiosity, maintaining engagement, etc.).

Delivery of blended / online instruction:

Learn how to customize the learning experience for learners. This includes getting to know your learners, selecting the best learning format (blended, fully online, f2f, synchronous or asynchronous), facilitating live instruction, orchestrating student interactions, fostering active engagement, guiding their pace, tracking learner progress, using formative assessment data to intervene, extend or reteach, and providing timely/constructive feedback.

Karen pipes up from the other end of the conference table, "The one aspect of The New Learning Ecosystem that we did not get into a lot of detail with when we introduced The New Learning Ecosystem was the idea of virtualization of instruction. I think that the situation that we face right now, with the uncertainty around education caused by the pandemic requires a robust discussion about virtualizing our instruction. As I think about how to proceed with The New Learning Ecosystem in the age of a pandemic, I believe the virtualization of learning is a cornerstone of that effort. If there is one thing that we can do immediately to work toward a radically learner-centered education in the age of COVID-19, it is to virtualize learning. Virtualization of learning does not mean that we are creating a cyber school or starting to compete in the cyber school world. The virtualization of learning is more essential and fundamental. Every learning experience that is created, whether learners engage in face-to-face, virtual, or blended, must be 'stored' in a virtual setting. By doing so, we allow our learners to access the learning experience at their convenience. This is particularly important when learners need to review a lesson or check their progress—they have the chance to "go back in time" and learn at their own pace. You also give teachers more options to create and modify their lessons and those of other teachers. By virtualizing learning, you position your school system to be adaptable. Teachers can use virtualized learning experiences in many different learning environments. Once the content is virtualized, teachers will find that learning is easier to stretch beyond the confines of their classroom and incorporate the community in which the learners live. Simply put, virtualization of learning positions the entire school system to be radically learner-centered. When a teacher creates learning experiences in a virtual format, the opportunities for learners increases. When virtualized, the teacher can use the learning experience in many ways other than in a traditional classroom...although that is still an option."

Everyone at the table is nodding their head in agreement. The last point is a key takeaway. Reiterating that learners are going to see teachers in a face-to-face setting makes it comfortable and easier for administrators to adopt the virtual piece of The New Learning Ecosystem.

PERFORMANCE-BASED LEARNING

Performance-based learning is based on the learner being able to do a specific task because of instruction. A performance-based system allows learners flexibility to progress through a curriculum at their own pace, reaching specific learning tasks aligned to the curriculum.

Craig stands up and looks at the drawing on the whiteboard. Rob could almost see the wheels turning in his head. "I think we should also look at the barriers of time and space as it relates to our current crisis situation. Time serves as the governing philosophy of education; it affects where learners learn, what learners learn, and how learners learn. School systems are organized as a place to warehouse learners based on their age—a form of time. Younger learners are placed in elementary schools, and older learners are placed in middle and high schools. They are placed in these buildings based on the randomness of their birthdate. The curriculum that learners are exposed to is determined to a great extent on their age. Depending on the particular school system, a learner is exposed to classes in a certain progression. For example, Biology is taught to all ninth-grade learners, while Algebra is taught to eighth-grade learners. The decision of when a learner is exposed to a concept or a class has nothing to do with their preparedness for the content. Rather, it is based on factors centered on adult convenience, for example, how old the student must be for compulsory education in the public schools, whether that decision comes from national, state, or local political forces. The birthdate of the learner determines their learning cohort, or grade level for their entire academic career. Time also dictates the speed in which the learner progresses through the curriculum. In the outdated learning ecosystem, teachers are encouraged to 'cover' the curriculum in a specific time period of a school year. Whether or not the learners actually learn the content is irrelevant to the importance of 'getting through' the entire curriculum. Adult, administrative convenience trumps the needs of the learner. This worked once upon a time—but not today, not anymore."

As Craig works his way back to his seat, Rob tells a story reminding the leadership team of a trip they made to another school that had been working on becoming learner-centered.

"Do you remember the trip we took to Hainestown elementary school last year? Hainestown has no grade levels or grades, and 'time' does not dictate the learning. Learners are regrouped every twelve days based on their needs relative to the concepts they are learning. The resulting learning environments, or 'classrooms,' are diverse with learners from different ages learning together because they are at a similar skill level on the relevant concept in the curriculum. Learners are not moved through the curriculum based on their age or where the school or the state tells them to be. The school believes in a performance-based system where learners show mastery on one concept before moving to the next concept."

Jane is writing something in her notebook. As she finishes, she asks, "Remember our takeaway from the visit? It was a significant paradigm shift for all of us to see a school in action that is based on the philosophy of being 'radically learner-centered.' Hainestown does not allow adult convenience to interfere with the learning experiences of the learner. When the system of learning is aligned to the idea of being radically learner-centered, then the notion of time shifts from being a barrier to learning to one where time is an asset to use in creating learning experiences that allow learners to master concepts. A paradigm shift away from making decisions for the school based on adult convenience and making the decisions based on being radically learner-centered is exactly what we need right now."

There is no exaggerating the effect the visit had on the leadership team. For months, the team had discussed the changes they wanted to make in the schools, but it was an intellectual exercise. It was so powerful to visit a physical school and witness what the team had been talking about actually being done in the real world. To speak to kids, parents, teachers, and support staff and see their passion for what they were doing filled the team with hope and promise. After visiting this school, the leadership team left with renewed optimism and confidence. The realization that a school can change to be radically learner-centered created a sense of urgency to go back to their district and start the necessary work to change their school district.

When Rob was done with his story, Craig starts to discuss the second barrier, "The second barrier that governs our schools is 'space.' The industrial age model of education is explicit in the fact that learning only happens in the school building itself. Furthermore, learning must always be monitored by a state-approved adult who determines whether or not a learner has progressed satisfactorily through the approved curriculum. The space issue is insidious in its influence within the old education ecosystem. Since the school system is predicated on the factory model, all systems associated with learning have their origin in the factory model of learning. Much like raw material moves through the factory floor from one station to the next, students move in batches from one class to the next. Bells determine when students and adults, can move from one place to another. In today's COVID-19 educational environment, space is no longer a fixed asset. For the safety of students, staff, and society, we are being asked to reimagine education and make space flexible. Learning can and will exist outside the school walls. It is our job to have the courage of our convictions and figure out how to deliver a quality education to our learners with space being a flexible variable."

"I agree," Rob says. "Now, more than ever, we must embrace the fact that learning does not have to be conducted within the walls of a school building. There can be a robust debate about whether you agree where the best learning can take place, but in today's crisis, we must open ourselves up to the fact that we must ensure that instruction is designed for different locations so that education becomes modular for our learners."

The conversation among the leadership team over the past two hours has been great and Rob feels as if the team is refocused on The New Learning Ecosystem instead of simply "survival mode." In acute times of crisis, leaders must help make sense of the world for their staff. Luckily for Rob, the groundwork for The New Learning Ecosystem has been laid over the past three years, and the leadership team just has to use that structure to help create the conditions for the best education experience for the learners as possible during the times of COVID-19.

Rob decides to add something as the group is standing up from the table and walking toward the door. "Let's remember the three takeaways from our discussion today. First, we are refocusing on The New Learning Ecosystem as a structure to help us navigate the COVID-19 crisis. Second, we must always be cognizant of and push against the tendency to lean into adult convenience instead of being learner-centered. Finally, let's reimagine what school can be during the pandemic (and beyond) by acting upon our paradigm shift toward becoming radically learner-centered. If we can do these three things, we will not only survive the turmoil caused by the pandemic, and we will come out the other side a better organization."

Rob remembers those early days when the leadership team was introducing The New Learning Ecosystem. Since then, the school district has made tremendous progress toward becoming radically learner-centered. The staff has embraced empowerment for both themselves and their students. The community is contributing to learning experiences for all learners in all grade levels. Most importantly, the school board declared that it was "non-negotiable" that the school district will become radically learner-centered—and they put their money where their mouth was. Now, during the biggest crisis in the history of public education, was not the time to stray from their vision. The New Learning Ecosystem offers the new structure needed to thrive during the COVID-19 crisis.

BOOK STUDY QUESTIONS FOR CHAPTER 1

1. In what ways is your school radically learner-centered right now?
2. What are the areas where you can become more learner-centered?
3. What are the activities or programs that your school does for learners that can lead to a more learner-centered environment?
4. In what ways can your school become less about adult convenience?
5. What are some of the everyday tasks that you do that reflect an adult convenience/command and control culture?
6. Think of three ways your school can begin to address the barriers of time.
7. Form a student action committee to ask them their thoughts on The New Learning Ecosystem. Report the results back to your book study group.

BOOKS

1. Disrupting Class by Clayton Christensen
2. Inevitable, Mass Customized Learning: Learning in the age of empowerment, (2012) by Chuck Schwahn and Bea McGarvey.
3. Beyond Reform, by The Lindsay Unified School District
4. Inevitable Too: Total Leaders Embrace Mass Customized Learning, by Chuck Schwahn and Bea McGarvey

WEB SITES:

1. Knowledge Works at https://knowledgeworks.org/
2. Getting Smart at *https://www.gettingsmart.com/*
3. Hackschooling Makes me Happy by Logan LaPlante. *https://youtu.be/h11u3vtcpaY*

4. The Lindsay Story: Confronting the Status Quo and Creating a New Vision for Learning. *https://youtu.be/jO2Zws8dOVw*
5. Design 39 Campus: http://www.design39campus.com/

CHAPTER 2
STAY TRUE TO YOURSELF

THE NEW LEADERSHIP REALITY

"To the person who does not know where he wants to go, there is no favorable wind."

—SENECA

CHAPTER 2 CONCEPTS AND THINK-ABOUTS

1. Your current reality and "magical thinking"
2. VUCA in the education world
3. A new VUCA-vision, understanding, clarity, and agility
4. A SAMR model for the post-COVID-19 education world

NO MAGICAL THINKING

"JANE, CAN YOU stay back for a little bit?" Rob asks Jane as she is almost out the door.

"Darn, I almost made it out the door!" Jane exclaims as she turns around and walks back to the conference table and sits in a chair. "So, what's up?" she asks Rob.

Rob walks to the door of the conference room and shuts it. He wants to run some ideas by her that are tumbling through his mind. He and Jane work well together because they complement each other. Jane has an ability to divine the underlying meaning of what Rob is trying to say. She helps him make sense of what is rolling around in his mind. Rob helps Jane think systemically about how to lead a school.

> ## VALUES
>
> Values are the things you think are important and help guide how you live and work.

"So, do you agree that refocusing on The New Learning Ecosystem and being purposeful about staying true to students, yourself, and staff are a way to help us through the crisis?" Rob begins as he takes a seat across the table from Jane.

"Yes, I agree," Jane answers, "During a crisis like this, our true values come out. All the work that the school district has done over the past three years toward becoming radically learner-centered is going to pay off. I also believe that it is important for school leaders to have a clear understanding about the present situation that we are in. Doing an environmental scan to realistically look at the changes occurring now and about to occur, is important for school leaders. I think it is important to understand our current situation. More than just reading the headlines on a news app on our phone, I think we have to study and think deeply about the current situation and how it will inform us for our future actions."

Jane looks across the table to make sure she has his attention and continues, "I was talking to the first-grade team on Zoom this morning, and they said something interesting. They seem to believe that once the immediate crisis is over that things will go back to the way it was before the crisis hit. In effect, they think our experiences now are just a temporary problem that just needs temporary solutions."

> ## VUCA
>
> VUCA is a way to help us understand the world. Leadership consists of making sense of the world in which we operate and then offering clarity for others around that understanding.

"That is fanciful thinking not at all based on our current reality and we cannot allow it to take hold in our schools or community. I have been working on a framework to understand our current situation, and I think it will help us figure out how we can proceed with our continued focus on becoming radically learner-centered." Rob stands up and walks to the whiteboard in the conference room.

"Okay, let's hear it," Jane says as Rob finishes cleaning the board.

"Have you ever heard of VUCA?" asks Rob.

"No, I haven't...the better question back to you is should I have heard about it before?" Jane retorts.

Rob writes V-U-C-A vertically down the left side of the white board in large letters and begins his explanation. "VUCA is something that has been around since the 1990s, but don't feel bad if you haven't heard much about it. I know that I just became aware of it recently myself. VUCA stands for volatility, uncertainty, complexity, and ambiguity. The acronym was developed by the Army War College to help them make sense of the post-Cold War world. The idea is that after World War Two, the world became ordered. Two sides were competing for geopolitical dominance, the Soviet Union and the United States. Although there was always some unpredictability, in general, you knew where the problems were going to arise, and you could use past practice to help you develop a solution to a current crisis. After the collapse of the Soviet Union and the Soviet satellite nations, the world became disordered and unpredictable. It became difficult, if not impossible, to make decisions using what happened in the past as a barometer to inform how you make sense of a new reality. In a nutshell, VUCA is summed up in this chart." Rob slides over a piece of paper to show Jane.

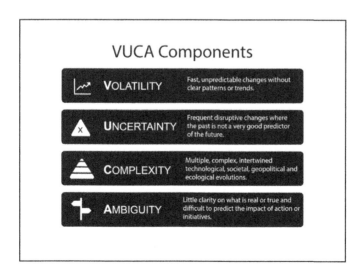

VUCA Components

VOLATILITY — Fast, unpredictable changes without clear patterns or trends.

UNCERTAINTY — Frequent disruptive changes where the past is not a very good predictor of the future.

COMPLEXITY — Multiple, complex, intertwined technological, societal, geopolitical and ecological evolutions.

AMBIGUITY — Little clarity on what is real or true and difficult to predict the impact of action or initiatives.

Jane leans back in her chair and studies the whiteboard as she takes in Rob's explanation. "I can see where this is really relevant to what we are facing right now," she says. "I know during the past few weeks, I've felt unmoored in the sense that it seemed like I was making a lot of decisions for the very first time in my career. There just didn't seem to be anything I could look back on in my principal experience that would help me make sense of the issues I was facing."

"That's exactly the crux of the VUCA framework. Let me read to you what I found on Wikipedia about the definitions of VUCA, and you tell me if it doesn't shine a light on our current situation." Rob takes a sheet of paper from his folder he carries with him. He writes the definition on the board.

> *"Volatility: the nature and dynamics of change, and the nature and speed of change forces and change catalysts.*
>
> *Uncertainty: the lack of predictability, the prospects for surprise, and the sense of awareness and understanding of issues and events.*
>
> *Complexity: the multiplex of forces, the confounding of issues, no cause-and-effect chain and confusion that surrounds organization.*
>
> *Ambiguity: the haziness of reality, the potential for misreads, and the mixed meanings of conditions; cause-and-effect confusion."*

"I get it," Jane says, "Remember last week when the leadership team spent the entire weekend working to create a plan to get instruction to our kids? We implemented the plan at 9:00 AM, and by 9:30, we had to scrap the whole thing because the secretary of education changed the rules around what was classified as instruction. That seems to me to be a textbook VUCA situation. The change came fast, it was unpredictable, it was a surprise, we could not see a cause and effect logic to the decision from the secretary of education and our best attempt at 'seeing' reality was an abysmal failure."

"I don't look at it as a failure, once you look at it through the lens of the VUCA framework," Rob retorted as he circled the VUCA definition. "We did the best we could with the information we had at the time. We also have to remember that there are counterpoints of the VUCA model that can help us navigate the complex world we are now facing."

Rob continues, "Let's look at how education has changed in the past few weeks." He returns to the whiteboard and draws another diagram.

PRE-COVID-19 AND POST-COVID-19 EDUCATIONAL STRUCTURES

"THIS IS WHAT the world looked like for educators in a pre-COVID-19 world. It was orderly and predictable. It kind of looked like this."

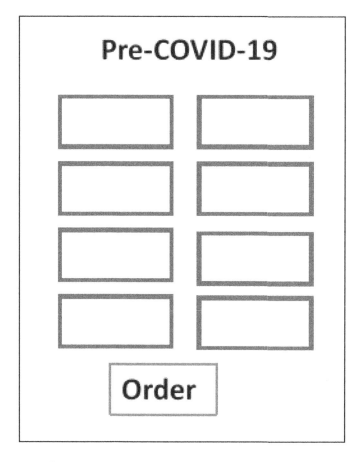

"That looks like our classrooms before we became radically learner-centered," Jane exclaimed, "I'm sure glad we don't look like that anymore!".

"Amen to that," Rob said, turning to look at Jane who had started to take notes in her notebook. "But the important point is that the education system in which all schools operated was in an orderly configuration. The number and types of decisions that leaders had to make every day were limited. For better or worse, the system of education created an orderly decision-making process. Now we add a significant variable called COVID-19 to our original model. In our case, the catalyst to change the system of education was the COVID-19 crisis, but you can imagine other disrupters having the same effect. Look at what that does to our orderly little world," Rob scratches some more drawings on the board and turns to give Jane an opportunity to see what he has drawn.

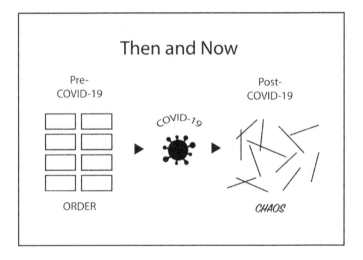

"You see, COVID-19 has introduced such a radical change that it has created chaos in the education system and its structures. Think about it. Overnight, traditional brick and mortar schools were forced to become online schools. Teachers who never thought they would teach online were forced to teach online. Learners found themselves learning online, which we know requires a different set of skills. Our learners are very adept at cruising through social media every day, which is what they are used to. Social media savvy does not equate to the skills needed to learn online. Parents, grandparents, aunts, uncles, and friends are suddenly forced to deal with the fact that school buildings are closed. The vast majority of all these educational stakeholders never considered the possibilities of mass school closings. The result is mass chaos with the people and the rapid destruction of the traditional educational structures." Rob pauses to catch his breath.

He's been thinking deeply about changing the structures of education for years. Still, he has had a hard time articulating them to people because there was no common frame of reference in which to engage in a conversation. Now that the crisis has forced a new

> ## EDUCATION STRUCTURES
>
> Education structures are the underlying assumptions that guide schooling. Grades, grade levels, master schedules are just a few examples of education structures.

frame of reference, Rob senses that now is a great time to talk about education structures.

"So, what do you think, Jane? Does any of this make sense to you?" Rob asks.

"It does," Jane answers, "But there is one thing I feel I have to say. I hear from our staff, parents, and students that once the Governor opens schools back up, everything will go back to the way it was before COVID-19 turned order into chaos as you have spelled it out on your chart. Do we really think our systems and structures of education will fundamentally change?"

"That's a great question, and I don't know if there is anyone that can answer that with 100% certainty in either direction," Rob says as he sits back down in the chair across from Jane, "So let's start with a question for you. Who is your best teacher?"

"You know the answer to that, Rob...it's easy, Chuck," answers Jane.

"Ok, I know Chuck. He is more of a traditional teacher, but he engages kids in such a way that he has them eating out of his hand in almost every lesson he teaches." Rob leans forward in his chair to make his point.

"Here is my question for you. Do you think Chuck would have welcomed teaching online without the crisis we are now experiencing? Of all the possible instructional strategies that he would have chosen before the crisis, where do you think online, virtual instruction would have been ranked in his mind?"

"Not high at all on his radar screen," Jane responds.

MY TWO CENTS

Understanding the leadership reality is necessary whether there is a crisis or not. Utilizing vision, understanding, clarity and agility will help build your leadership muscles regardless of the situation.

"Exactly," Rob says, "During this crisis, the possibilities of instruction, content, and communication are being expanded because people are forced into trying new and uncomfortable things. I am not saying that Chuck is ever going to want to teach in a 100% online format. What I am saying is that the possibilities open for him to expand his instructional toolbox have now expanded drastically. The discussion of how the content is best learned by the learner can now take precedent. In the pre-COVID-19 world, there was not a lot of talk about what is the best learning modality for learners because the toolbox of most teachers was not robust enough. Because of this crisis, teacher's instructional toolboxes have expanded, and the important question of 'how is the content best learned' is deepened. Even when we go back into our schools, which we all hope is sooner rather than later, the subtle and not so subtle changes that teachers have experienced will change the structures of education. That is why I say that our assumption from this crisis is that things will never go back to the way they were before COVID-19 came along."

Rob fumbles through the papers in front of him. He always threatens to buy some sort of technology that will help him organize his thoughts when he is in meetings, but he never does. He settles for scribbling on scraps pieces of paper and praying that he can find what he is looking for. He finds the chart he is looking for and slides it across the table to Jane.

A NEW VUCA

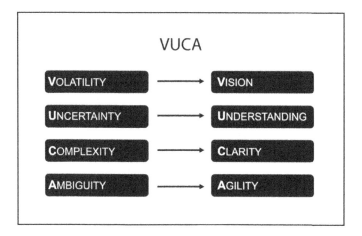

"The VUCA on the left of this chart helps us understand the world we are dealing with and gives us a framework in which to make sense of our leadership reality," Rob says. "The VUCA on the right side of the chart is a roadmap for action which will allow us to understand the short-term reality, but also the long-term reality we want to create. I have scratched out some thoughts on the meaning of vision, understanding, clarity, and agility as it relates to our situation." Rob gets up from the table and walks back over to the whiteboard and quickly draws a four-square matrix.

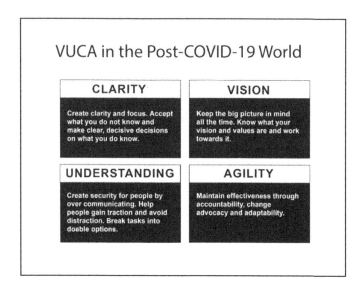

"I can see why you want to double down on our vision for The New Learning Ecosystem," Jane says. "We have done so much work on creating a vision for the school district and working on living our values that I can see that if we keep these topics 'top of mind' that decision making will be clearer. Maybe not less complex, but clearer. I'm thinking of the Roy Disney quote that is hanging in our Board room, 'It's not hard to make decisions when you know what your values are.'"

"Exactly!" Rob replies. "Living our vision for the school district and our learners is essential right now. The hard work our staff, school board, and community put into creating a vision is being put into great use right now. Let's keep in mind the question that helped us create our vision: 'What will we look like, feel like, and be like when we are operating at our ideal best?'"

Rob walks back to his chair, grabs the back of the chair, and asks Jane, "What is your take on the 'understanding' part of the matrix?"

Jane shifts in her chair a little before she answers. "Well, I think of something I have heard John Maxwell say about leading through a crisis. He says that a crisis causes distractions for the people that work for you. A leader's job is to provide traction in a world of distraction. I like the mental image that provides. I have tried to be transparent with people as I have had to make decisions since the schools were closed to let them know that I am making the decision based on the best information I have right now. Maybe the rules will change in two minutes, but as of this minute, this is the decision that I am making. I think people appreciate the fact that you are making a decision and will cut you some slack if the decision must be reversed because the ground rules changed in some way. I also have seen instances where people appreciate that a leader can break down complex tasks into doable parts. By giving people concrete, doable tasks, they feel as if they are contributing to a larger good, and the world does not seem so crazy."

"I love that point Jane," Rob replies. "Herb Kelleher, the founder of Southwest Airlines, once said 'think small to get big' and I believe that meant it is easy to get overwhelmed with the magnitude of what you want to achieve, or in our case, the situation we are facing. Doing something, no matter how small, is better than doing nothing at all. As the old saying goes, 'the best time to plant a tree was 20 years ago, the second-best time is now.'"

"No worries, Rob," Jane says. She thinks to herself that it is not at all uncommon for "simple" ideas to morph into bigger ones when Rob is involved.

As Rob's last comments float in the air, Jane considers the mindset change the leadership team had to make to become less risk averse. People holding leadership positions today

LEADERSHIP TEAM

You will see "leadership team" used a lot in this story. A leadership team is a group of leaders in a school or school district that are brought together by a leader to help make decisions and set the vision for the organization.

have come up through a system of education that rewards compliance and discourages risk taking. Accountability measures that started with No Child Left Behind in 2002 accelerated throughout the 2010s. When your job depends on how well students do on tests scores and how well the rules of accountability are followed, it is exceedingly difficult to think outside the box. Today's leaders in education were promoted because of their ability to successfully navigate accountability and compliance issues. The leadership team changed their risk averse mindset by starting to take small risks. Once they were comfortable with the smaller risks, they felt more comfortable taking larger ones. Rob made sure that any risk was within the zone of acceptable loss and would lead their school toward the vision of the school district. Jane is brought back to the present conversation with Rob when she notices that he has gotten up from his chair and has been writing on the one small corner of the whiteboard that is still blank.

"Jane, do you remember the SAMR model that Dr. Ruben Puentedura developed for technology integration into schools?" Rob asks.

"I vaguely remember parts of it," Jane answers truthfully.

"Great, I'll start by giving you a definition of the SAMR model based on Wikipedia." Rob reads from a piece of paper in his hand. "'SAMR is an acronym that stands for Substitution, Augmentation, Modification, and Redefinition. The SAMR model provides a technique for moving through degrees of technology adoption to find more meaningful uses of technology in teaching and move away from simply using tech for tech's sake.' Now, that is the definition. I want to adjust the acronym slightly to help us make meaning of the current world of education. Let me know what you think."

LEARNER-CENTERED INSTRUCTION DURING A CRISIS

ROB HAS FINISHED writing on the whiteboard.

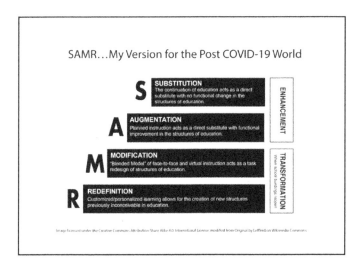

Rob began, "Think back to what it was like for us a few weeks ago when we were considering how to transition to an online school overnight—wow! Never mind the logistics of making sure all kids had an equal opportunity to get the education, but do you remember the overwhelming feeling we all experienced when trying to get this figured out?"

"Oh, yes I do," Jane answers. "The schools closing on such short notice created all sorts of problems—not the least of which was that we did not have school that day, so none of our teachers or learners had their materials. Ugh! I'm glad we got that figured out!"

"Those logistics were bad enough," Rob continued, "but don't forget that once we had those things figured out, we had to start thinking about guaranteeing quality instruction to our learners. That is why the modified SAMR model helps us as we move forward to think of the different stages we are experiencing in this journey. In the first stage, which is what you were describing, Jane, it was like triage. We just wanted to get something out to the learners as fast as we could. If you remember, the Department of Education was sending out mixed messages to the field as they were struggling to keep up with the situation too. I think at the end of the day, our first 'go' at changing education in this crisis falls under 'substitution.' We were only concerned with taking what we were usually doing in the classroom and getting that content, in any format, online, paper and pencil packets, or carrier pigeon, to the kids."

Jane laughs at Rob's statement as she stops copying Rob's modified SAMR model in her notebook, "I'm chuckling at your carrier pigeon comment. I think that might have been an option late one night when we were trying to figure this out!"

"Tell me about it! Once the first shock to the system was over, and we realized that schools were going to be closed for more than the original two weeks, we started to plan for how we can augment instruction. It was just last week after the teachers received their first five hours of professional learning on effective virtual instruction that we felt comfortable asking the question, 'How can we deliver even better instruction and content now than we were before COVID-19?' I started to get some feedback late last week that our staff is embracing that challenge. That's thanks to all of you and your hard work. You have built such good relationships with your staff that you can ask these types of tough questions and feel pretty confident that they will respond well."

Jane replies, "I can see where we have gone through the 'substitute' and 'augment' stages. I also want to refocus on the clarity, vision, and agility squares that determine an effective response to a VUCA world. It seems like your SAMR model provides those three things, clarity, vision, and agility. So, how will we tackle the next stages of the adapted SAMR model? I see from the chart on the wall it means we will move from enhancement to transformation. What does that look like?"

> ## BLENDED MODEL
>
> Blended model of instruction occurs when a learner receives instruction in both a face to face and online environment.

"It looks like what our vision for education has been all along with The New Learning Ecosystem. When our schools open back up, all of our staff will not only have had quality professional learning in delivering online content, something that has already started, but they will have actually worked in an online environment using what they have learned. It would have taken us years to accomplish the same thing under normal circumstances. We just did it in three weeks. When we come back, we must have a plan in place, so we don't squander what we have learned from the school closure. We can create a blended model of education that takes the best of face to face learning and the best of virtual learning and create a new structure of education for our learners. That will bring us one step closer to becoming radically learner-centered. We will modify the existing structure to create something new." Rob steps back from the board to study what he has written.

Jane gets up from her chair and joins Rob near the whiteboard. "As you know Rob, we have done some limited blended learning already with some teachers in a 'pilot program.' I can see us using what we learned from them, couple it with the experiences all of our teachers are having right now, to start creating a plan."

"I like the way you're thinking Jane," Rob chimes in. "We will have to plan purposefully and think hard about what we think the best route will be for expanding the pilot programs—because at the end of the day, 'modification' is not where we want to live. If we really believe in the idea of The New Learning Ecosystem and the act of becoming radically learner-centered, then we must get to 'redefinition.' Boy, that is a tall task. I was telling you earlier that I was getting overwhelmed thinking about how to get our systems and structures to the 'redefinition' stage so I went for a walk. You can thank a red-winged blackbird for helping to clarify something that we all know around this table. Regardless of how crazy it has been over the past few weeks, we mustn't lose sight of our ultimate goal, which is to become radically learner-centered through The New Learning Ecosystem."

PARALYSIS BY ANALYSIS

THE PHONE IN the conference room rings and Rob answers. After shaking his head a few times, he says, "Sure, I'll take it in my office."

"I'm sorry about this, but Ben is on the phone. You know how close our two school districts are, and he wants to pick my brain about some things as he and his school district strategize about their next steps. Thank you, Jane, for helping me talk through the SAMR idea. I think it will help us as we figure out how to reopen schools."

Jane walks over to the table and picks up her notebook. "No problem, Rob. I'll put some more thought into it and if I think of anything interesting, I'll give you a call."

"That will be great, Jane. Thank you!" Rob replies.

He turns off the lights in the conference room and walks down the hallway to his office. As he gets closer to his office, a sense of gloom comes over him. He likes Ben and knows that Ben wants to do what's best for kids, but Ben just can't get out of his own way sometimes. Ben over analyzes every decision, which, often, creates a "paralysis by analysis" situation. On top of all of that, Rob can't help but think of a saying whenever he talks to Ben, "It's hard to learn something when you already know everything." With all these thoughts in mind, Rob walks into his office, shuts the door and reaches for the phone.

"Hey Ben, what's new in your world? I can't imagine there's much new!" Rob likes to break the ice with a little teasing.

"Hello Rob, you know better than that...it's been as nuts in your school district as it's been in mine. It has been crazy here. I feel like I can hardly keep up. I called because I want to run something by you."

"Sure, go right ahead, I'm all ears," Rob replies as he settles into his chair.

"Have you seen the latest guidance from the Department of Education on how to educate our kids during this crisis?" Ben asks.

"Sure, I perused it briefly this morning...it didn't seem like there was anything in there that would prevent us from doing what we want to do in our district," Rob answers.

"I wish we were so lucky!" Ben replies, "I looked into the footnotes that guided their suggestions, and footnote 3.2a clearly interferes with our district policy number 134.3a (AR). If I do what they suggest, then I will break local Board policy!"

"Now, hold on a minute Ben," Rob replies, "I take the word 'suggest' seriously from the Department of Ed. I don't think they are interested during these unprecedented times of crisis to tell any school district what they have to do. There are just too many moving parts. Each school district is so unique in their challenges, weaknesses, and strengths that I don't believe the Department of Education meant that document to be anything more than helpful suggestions."

"Are you telling me you are ignoring the suggestions?" asks Ben.

"Ignoring is probably not the right word. The guidance is suggestions, after all. I believe strongly that they are not meant to be our marching orders. Besides, I am more concerned about doing what is right for all our kids right now, and we'll let the bureaucracy catch up to us." Rob answers.

"Well, we did conduct four surveys of our community according to Board policy 199.34, and the results were split 50/50 with the two options we gave the community for how we are going to proceed with educating our kids during this crisis. On top of that, some of the suggestions by the Department of Education go against school code section 915-A. I know this because I called our district solicitor three times today to talk about it. One last thing: I heard that one of our local State representatives is going to introduce a Bill that will loosen some of the testing restrictions on schools. I am just not comfortable with that-"

Rob interrupts Ben, "I am sure you are not comfortable, and maybe I'm not either because everything that is happening makes us feel like we have no control. But we have to embrace the lack of control in these volatile times. Ben, I am living in an uncomfortable professional situation too. Still, I always fall back to what our vision for our school district is and how we can get there, regardless of policies or pandemics! Tell me, Ben, what do you want for your school district?"

"We surveyed all 18 different stakeholder groups last year. I had a hard time making sense of the data in light of school board policy number 1093.8.c-1, which says that there must be a clear consensus from surveys if we are to use the results to guide decisions in the district. There was just not any clear consensus."

"I remember that policy, Ben. Didn't you propose that to the Board three years ago?" asks Rob.

"I did," answers Ben, "I just wanted to make sure that all of the data that we used was agreed upon by the district stakeholders and..."

At this point in the conversation, Rob starts to zone out. This often happens when Rob talks to Ben. There is not a lot of "substance" to Ben in the sense that he never lets people know what his vision of education, learning, and leadership is. He hides behind policies and surveys. Some can get away with that leadership style for most of their careers until a crisis like this occurs, then the lack of a foundational substance will come to light.

Rob focuses back in on Ben's conversation, "...so I am going to recommend that my district does not change anything in how we are delivering curriculum and instruction to our kids and we will keep things status quo."

"Okay," Rob just has to ask one more question, "but aren't your learners only getting about 20 minutes of instruction a day right now?"

"Yes, but that is the best we can do when considering appropriate Board policies, guidance from the Department of Education, and advice from our solicitor."

"So, Ben, did I answer the question that led to your call?" Rob gently tries to put an end to the phone call.

"I just need to know what you are going to do in the next two weeks with your learners."

"We are going to transform the way our entire school system educates kids over the next six months, and it starts today. As a matter of fact, the leadership team already met to get things rolling," Rob answers with a slight grin.

"You're nuts, but good luck with all of that 'transformation,'" says Ben.

"Thank you, Ben, take care." Rob hangs up the receiver. Every conversation with Ben always leads to the same conclusion for Rob: Ben just can't get out of his own way!

> ## My Two Cents
>
> Don't be Ben. Do not overanalyze and paralyze yourself by hiding behind policy and procedure. Leadership takes courage. Do what you know is right for you learners! Remember: it's easier to ask for forgiveness than ask for permission!

Rob places the receiver of the phone down and takes a deep breath. Being timid is not going to help kids and families during this crisis.

Brett knocks on the door and peeks his head in. "I heard you were on the phone with Ben. How's he doing?"

"Oh, I figure about the same as usual. Pouring over his policies and survey data right now. He'll get everything figured out, I suppose. So, where were we in our conversation?" Rob asks.

Brett chuckles a little. The difference in leadership style between Ben and Rob is night and day. Rob's passion which is grounded in a strong vision for learning contrasts sharply with Ben's analytical leadership style that revolves around data. Brett's happy that Rob is the superintendent of his school district right now and not Ben. The flexibility that comes from knowing and trusting yourself will serve Rob, Brett, and the school district well in the upcoming months.

BOOK STUDY QUESTIONS FOR CHAPTER 2

1. What "magical thinking" is driving your decision-making process right now?
2. How has your school communicated the new leadership reality to your staff, students, and community?
3. How can the SAMR model be used to help communicate your long-term goals for the school district?
4. Write down your vision for your school or school district. How does your vision help create understanding and clarity for your staff and other stakeholders?
5. Convene a group of students, a group of staff, and a group of parents and share your vision for your school or school district with them. After you have facilitated each group, reflect on

what you learned from them. Did what you learn make you adjust your vision at all?

BOOKS

1. High Output Management by Andrew Grove
2. Man's Search for Meaning by Viktor Frankl
3. The Fifth Discipline by Peter Senge
4. Leading Change by John Kotter
5. Nuts! Southwest Airlines Crazy Recipe for Business & Personal Success by Kevin Freiberg and Jackie Freiberg

WEB SITES

1. (Day 1) Leading Through Crisis: A Virtual Leadership Summit with John C. Maxwell: *https://youtu.be/H7MGO6C5r18*

CHAPTER 3
STAYING TRUE TO YOURSELF

CRISIS DECISION MAKING

"What is important is seldom urgent and what is urgent is seldom important."

—PRESIDENT DWIGHT EISENHOWER (ATTRIBUTED)

CHAPTER 3 CONCEPTS AND THINK-ABOUTS

1. The urgent/important matrix
2. Leading during a crisis
3. Your non-negotiable value statements for learning and leadership
4. Creating your leadership philosophy

Rob gets out of his car at the high school and grins. The student parking lot is half empty—or, perhaps he should say, half full. It's been three years since the COVID-19 crisis upset the education world and a lot has changed in Rob's school district.

"Three years ago, we were spending a lot of time and effort trying to figure out a lottery system for student parking passes. I'm so glad we don't have to waste our time worrying about that anymore," Rob thinks to himself.

In the distance, he hears the familiar song of a red-winged blackbird. Rob has been paying more attention to those birds ever since his walk outside his office three years ago. The song from the red-winged blackbird and the resulting revelation set the school district on a path to where it is today.

"Those were some crazy days," Rob thinks as he walks toward the high school entrance. The shock three years ago of becoming an "online" school overnight and the resulting upheaval in the school structures has been the leadership challenge of his career. He's been threatening to write a book about his experiences but hasn't gotten around to it yet. Maybe someday.

He swipes his school district identification card to gain access to the school building. He notices how nicely the new card reader system works. The system was put in place last year to allow access for students and staff as they come and go into the building. There was some consternation about having students swipe as they entered every classroom for office hours, but once everyone saw how it helped make The New Learning Ecosystem come alive, most hesitation went away. The system automatically populates the school district's student information system to track attendance—which eliminates manual attendance taking and gives time back to the teachers.

He says "hello" to the main office staff as he passes by—a habit he's kept up since his early days as an educator. A veteran teacher once told him that the secretaries and the custodial staff are the ones you need to get to know because they really know how to get things done in the school. So far, that advice has never steered him wrong. Getting the office staff involved in The New Learning Ecosystem allowed the entire district to become radically learner-centered and adopt the changes faster than he had anticipated.

Rob see Craig in his office, so knocks on the door.

"I thought you might be a little early for today's meeting," Craig says with a grin. Today's presentation has specially-invited VIP guests.

Ever since the school district changed the way it "did school," there have been hundreds of educators, politicians, and community members visiting the district to learn the story of how they became radically learner-centered. There have been so many requests that Rob and the leadership team had to create a schedule for two tours a month to streamline the process and help visitors learn what they needed to know to get started in their own districts—and they've been booking six months in advance.

Rob leans on the doorway. "Yes, I am excited by this visit. The United States Secretary of Education is coming with their entourage, so that's a big deal. I like the fact that we also included some of the requests from smaller school districts so they can interact with the Secretary and maybe get some conversation going between them. Do we have everything ready?"

"Yes, sir," answers Craig. "Jane is down in the room making sure everything is in place, and I just finished some updates on the data we track."

"What does it look like? I noticed the student parking lot is about half full, so that is a positive sign," Rob said.

Craig turns in his chair and takes a piece of paper from the printer that sits behind him. He studies the paper before he answers. "Great observation. I think we are figuring out how to manage the challenge of mixing our face to face learning, hybrid learning, office hours, and community learning opportunities. Today we are scheduled for 48% of our students to be in the building taking seminars, courses, or meeting with teachers during their office hours. Of that 48%, 70% are coming to school during what we used to call 'normal school hours' of 7:30-3:00. The rest are taking advantage of the flex time from 4:00-8:00 to come into the school for their classes. Of the 52% not in the building today, 30% of them are in one of the apprentice programs we organized with the Chamber of Commerce and the Main Street Committee, another 40% are engaged in internships, and 20% are participating in a week-long job shadowing program. The final 10% are in various stages of working on their community projects." Craig states with no small amount of satisfaction.

"That is outstanding!" Rob replies. "You fought so hard to make the community an integral part of The New Learning Ecosystem with apprentices, internships, job shadowing experiences, and projects. It is perfect for our community and the needs of our students.

"As proud as I am of those accomplishments, I appreciate the point you make to school districts that come to visit. You always tell them that what works for our community and us may not work for their community. A true Learning Ecosystem must be customized to the students and community. By the way, have you heard from Carol lately?" Carol is a superintendent from a school district in the region.

"It's funny you should ask," Craig answers as he puts his data sheet in a folder, "I visited their school yesterday—boy are they moving! Since their community infrastructure isn't as robust as ours, they have formed partnerships with manufacturing organizations and local businesses to provide learning opportunities for their students. I watched a trainer from the Hardwood Lumber Association give a lesson on algebra from the back of a tri-axle log truck. It was unbelievable."

Rob thinks back to the first-time Carol came to visit his school district with her leadership team. Her school district is about 100 miles away and is significantly more rural than Rob's district. She approached the visit to their district with a growth mindset. Instead of looking at just the obstacles of becoming learner-centered, she was focused on how they could adapt the approach for her district. Rob always tells the tour groups that action is the most vital part of change—not merely following along and reacting. Action, plus the desire to change the educational structures to become radically learner-centered is the key to success and lasting change.

"Why haven't I thought of teaching from a log truck, Craig?" Rob jokes. "I would love to see that someday! In the meantime, let's make our way down to the room and wait for our guests to arrive." Rob and Craig leave the office together and make their way to the room where the presentation will occur, discussing other highlights they want to bring up to their special guests today.

LEADERSHIP DECISIONS DURING A CRISIS

FORTY-FIVE MINUTES LATER, after welcoming everyone to the tour and introducing the leadership team, Rob launches into the presentation. His part of the tour is to tell the story of how the COVID-19 crisis became a catalyst for the changes in his school district that the audience has come to see.

"There are a few core tenets you will hear about today that our school district lives by and these tenets keep everyone focused on our mission. One of the most important is, 'Don't waste a crisis.' A crisis is a time when assumptions are questioned. People are forced to think outside the box. In many cases, you are forced to draw a new box while floating through the air. At least that is how we felt during the few months of the COVID-19 related school crisis. We can remember those first few months as the most hectic of our careers. As the leadership team met two, three, or even four times a day during those crazy times, we started to get a sense that we were missing something. As a group, we felt unmoored from our mission. It took some work to get us back on track, but we did it. I want to share with you how we did that."

Rob looks at the crowd. He has done this part of the presentation so many times that he doesn't need notes and he's able to concentrate on the reaction of the crowd. He knows that the Secretary only has two hours precious hours to spend, so he wants to make sure the hard work of the staff, the learners, and the community comes across to the audience.

"The most difficult thing to do in any crisis, but especially one as severe as the COVID-19 crisis, is to 'slow down' your day. When I say slow down, what I mean to say is that it is easy to get into the trap of making snap decisions without consideration for the long-term ramifications of the decision on your school, students, staff, or the community. It's challenging to differentiate the decisions that are less important from those that are more important for your school, students, and staff when everyone is constantly in a reactive crisis-mode. Often the decisions that we do not treat purposefully are the ones that we have to revisit after they don't work out the way we think they should. They're the ones that end up haunting us once the initial shock from the crisis starts to wear off."

URGENCY MATRIX

ROB NODS TO Jane and she projects a matrix on the screen. "As a leadership team, we went back to our basic understandings about leadership and management. One of the seminal works over the last thirty years, as you know, is the work of Stephen R. Covey. Now, there is a lot that we can take from his book The 7 Habits of Highly Effective People, but the one that helped us 'slow down' our decision making was the urgent/important matrix you see behind me."

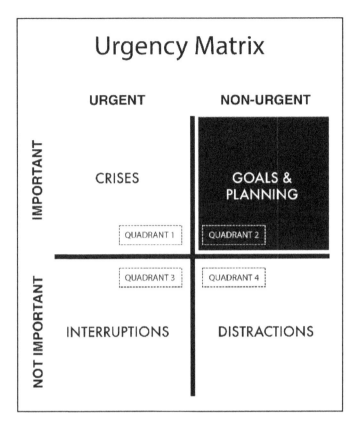

"Our leadership team took the time, even in the middle of the COVID-19 crisis, to reflect on this matrix. We considered the work and the pressures we were under at the time, and how all of that impacted the school district's goals and vision for our learners—and not just what we needed to do to survive. Some of my colleagues in the superintendent world thought we were crazy to spend time on what they considered unnecessary conversations when there were more important things to discuss. I told them then and now: reflecting on this matrix begins the most important conversations you will ever have for your school district."

Rob pauses to make sure the final point is sinking in. He and the leadership team know that the conversations triggered by the matrix laid the foundation for their work over the past three years—and it was the key to their success in building lasting change.

Craig makes eye contact with Rob and indicates he'd like to speak. This isn't part of their staged tour, but Rob trusts Craig. He's come a long way since those early days of his career when public speaking made him nervous and you'd be hard pressed to get him to voice an opinion on anything in a group setting. The saying that "a crisis shows the true grit of a leader" is true in Craig's case as he's grown into his leadership role and now confidently asserts his thoughts.

Craig works his way to the front of the room and says, "I am going to barge in here a little bit. I know it's important for you to hear from a 'front line' leader at this point. Rob is right when he says the leadership team took this conversation very seriously. What we came to realize is that leaders prioritize decisions every day. Even if Covey's framework is not top of mind, school leaders have different buckets in which they place their decisions. Regardless of how we prioritized decisions in the past, the COVID-19 crisis forced us to re-prioritize. Things we thought were earth-shatteringly important pre-COVID-19, were not so important anymore. Our definition of 'busy work' and 'time-wasters' significantly changed. As a leadership team, we became aware of the re-prioritization and made a point to remind ourselves every day that we were in a time of constant fluidity and that we couldn't use the same decision-making process that worked in the past. As a leadership team, we met to review the decisions that we made in the first three weeks of the crisis and placed them in the matrix so we could address each according to priority. We also thought back to decisions 'pre-COVID-19' and compared to how different the matrix looked."

Craig nods at Jane, and she projects the next slide. "On the screen, you'll see the questions that we asked ourselves during leadership team meetings to help us be aware of the decision-making changes forced on us by the crisis. We started in the lower right-hand corner of the matrix.

I know this is a presentation faux-pas, but I'm going to literally read from the screen because this information is so important."

He reads from the screen, "Quadrant Number Four not urgent/not important:

1. What are the items that have now become "busy work" and are not contributing to our vision of the school and reflecting our value statements about learning and leadership?
2. What are the distractions in our new work-life that do not allow us to live our value statements?"

He looks away from the screen and adds, "We will talk to you about how we created our value statements in a little while. For now, just remember that our individual professional value statements were an important factor in answering these questions."

As Jane advances the presentation, Craig continues, "Quadrant Number Three urgent/not important:

1. In our COVID-19 leadership climate, it seemed like everything was an interruption. Our rate of decision making increased so much that it seemed we did not have the time to not be interrupted! At this point, we remembered that there had been a reordering of priorities and how we worked. Items that we thought were important in our pre-COVID-19 world, simply were not important anymore. What are those items for you and your school?
2. How have our value statements shifted what we believe to be important or not important?"

Craig continues, "Quadrant Number One urgent/important: School leaders spent so much time in this quadrant during the crisis some probably wanted to redecorate the place! Let's just take a minute to wallow in the fact that we had to spend time in this quadrant to keep our schools afloat. Have you had enough 'wallow' time? We sure did.

Let's look at some of the decisions that we are placing in this quadrant and decide if some of them can be redirected to other quadrants. This was such an important exercise for the leadership team. We used the new school leadership reality, coupled with our value statements to determine where decisions need to be placed.

1. Is what you are answering or deciding upon really a crisis (as defined in our new world) or an interruption or a distraction?
2. Can something that is genuinely a crisis be leveraged and moved to Quadrant Number Two?"

Craig looks back at the audience and watches them ponder what issues they could have organized differently.

Rob stands back up. "Thank you, Craig, for reviewing these first three quadrants." Rob looks at the audience. "I hope the commitment and passion our leadership team undertook to answer these questions came through in Craig's explanation of the first three quadrants."

"I want to finish this part of the presentation to talk about Quadrant Number Two. In most ways, the work of re-prioritization centered on thinking deeply about this quadrant. The reason we felt this work was so important is the leadership team believed this quadrant is where the growth, vitality, and sustainability of our school district occurs. While making decisions based on the first three quadrants may keep our schools functional in the short-term, working in Quadrant Number Two guarantees the long-term survival of our schools. In this quadrant, we looked for decisions that strategically lead to the goals of the leadership team, the community, staff, and students have for the school. We came to believe in times of severe crisis, that this is the quadrant where we wanted to spend most of our time.

Next, we'll go into detail about how we did just a few things that allowed for a focus on learning, leadership, and a renewed commitment to our New Learning Ecosystem."

The day's agenda moved from the introductory presentation to a tour of the Innovation Lab. The Innovation Lab is a place where staff and students collaborate on projects. With help from local industry, the lab is a technology-rich creative space designed to enhance creative ideas. Rob led the Secretary of Education and her entourage down the hallway while the rest of the people in the group followed behind. Diane trails behind to introduce herself to a principal from another school who had come with his leadership team.

LEADERSHIP PHILOSOPHY

> ### LEADERSHIP PHILOSOPHY
>
> A leadership philosophy is a set of beliefs and principles that governs the actions of a leader. A leadership philosophy is created by synthesizing leadership experiences with theoretical knowledge

"Hello, I'm Diane, I am one of the middle school principals in the district. So, what do you think of your day so far?" asks Diane, as they walk toward the Innovation Lab together.

"It's been eye-opening, and I am looking forward to seeing the Innovation Lab. It's pretty cool to be here with the Secretary...by the way, my name is Curt."

"Nice to meet you Curt, is there anything you would like to ask me instead of asking in front of the group?"

Curt takes a few steps before he answers. "That's a good question. I understand the idea of Covey's four quadrants. I can imagine how difficult it was to re-prioritize decisions, especially at the height of the COVID-19 crisis. But this is what I am really wondering about, and maybe you can help me. During this morning's presentation, Rob and Craig talked about leadership value statements. How in the heck did you create those, and what staff were required to create them?" Curt asked.

Diane chuckles and says, "Fortunately, we have a long walk to the Innovation Lab, and I have a feeling that Rob will stop and show the Secretary some other things along the way, so I'll have time to answer your question. But first, you tell me: what is your school district's core leadership philosophy?"

"Um, I don't know if we have a concrete leadership philosophy. We talk about the work of Simon Sinek, John Maxwell, Jim Collins, among others. We take bits and pieces from each one and use what is relevant to our circumstances at the time," Craig says, a little sheepishly.

Diane stops and reaches out to stop Craig, as well. "Hey—that's outstanding! The fact that you are engaging in discussions about leadership is the first step in creating a leadership philosophy. Our district would not have been able to achieve all that we have achieved in the last three years without having those discussions about multiple leadership thought leaders ourselves and the bigger picture elements don't happen overnight. Our leadership team believes discussions like you are having is step one in the process of creating a leadership philosophy. The next step is to craft a specific philosophy to match your school, community, and leadership team. There is no wrong or right answer, the important thing is to do the work to create a philosophy. I will tell you about our philosophy, but by no means does it mean it is the 'right' answer or even close to the right answer for your team. My husband works in a district that embraced the "appreciate inquiry" philosophy, and they have done great work to create a great learning environment for their learners. The important thing is to create one."

The two principals continue their walk toward the innovation lab and Curt replies, "Yeah, I can see what you are saying. I think we are probably further along in creating a philosophy than I am letting on. We have done a lot of study around Clayton Christensen's Disrupting Class book and how our leadership team can lead disruption in our schools."

"Bingo!" answers Diane. "You're getting close. In our school district, we started by having everyone on the district leadership team create a non-negotiable value statement for leadership and a separate value statement for learning. Rob then tasked us to create a 'principal action team,' or PAT, from our

> ### NON-NEGOTIABLE VALUE STATEMENT
>
> A non-negotiable value statement articulates the leader's top priorities and makes a promise to the leader's community to commit to those priorities.

building staff, and we went through the same process with them. I'll tell you about our philosophy and how we used it to create our non-negotiable value statements for learning and leadership. Although the specific philosophy is different, the process of creating the non-negotiable statements is transferable to any philosophy you choose and guides your decisions from that point forward."

THREE LEADERSHIP BELIEFS ABOUT A CRISIS

DIANE CONTINUED, "To ground ourselves in the school leadership reality we faced, the leadership team created three core beliefs about the COVID-19 crisis. First, this crisis is unique. In a major crisis, there is no playbook for action. In a normal situation, a leader is informed by patterns of actions and situations that happened in the past. You can dig into your past experiences and remember what worked, and did not work, and adjust accordingly. A crisis has its own rules of engagement. In the case of a State-wide school closure, where do you even start? A leader will find oneself torn between making decisions too quickly and being overrun by events when taking too much time to decide. What we learned about VUCA was important in creating this first core value."

"VUCA-what?" asked Curt with a puzzled look on his face.

Diane laughed, "VUCA stands for volatility, uncertainty, complexity, and ambiguity." She then gives Curt a brief overview of the VUCA world and how the leadership team came to understand the reality of the situation as it existed amid the COVID-19 crisis.

"Ok, that makes a lot of sense," said Curt when Diane had finished her explanation. "So, what are your other core beliefs you created to help you get through the crisis?"

Diane smiled, "The second core belief is crises are fast-paced. In a crisis, the facts and situation change so rapidly that you find yourself constantly adjusting. A decision made at 9:00 AM that is logical and based on the best available information can be obsolete by 9:10 AM when new information comes to light. Shifting decision-making inputs are frustrating and difficult to prepare for. All of us knew intellectually that our decision-making pace had quickened, but it's hard to realize how much when you are drinking from the fire hose of information coming at you! Being cognitively aware of the quickened pace was helpful."

"I agree with that wholeheartedly," said Curt. "There were a few days early in the crisis where I felt the team in my district suffered from 'paralysis by analysis.' We overcame it, but it probably should have happened sooner."

"Same here in our district. Rob spends a lot of time thinking about these things, so we were a little ahead of the curve, but we had our days where it felt like we were just spinning our wheels, too." Diane shook her head as she remembered those times.

"I remember sitting home and feeling so alone at times, which happens to be our third belief about a crisis, namely that a crisis is isolating for leaders. The saying that 'it's lonely at the top' is amplified during a crisis. Often, information gets funneled to the top, or information is only given to the person at the top of the organization. When this happens, the perspective of the leader is different from those within the system because of the information they have at their disposal. People and stakeholders within your system may not understand the decisions you made because they are not aware of the context as well as you. We really concentrated on putting systems in place to communicate with each other at the leadership team level, the school building level, and the wider community. Those structures and systems were essential to creating a mutual understanding of the environment we all faced. Creating a shared understanding is important in building a harmonious leadership team whether the school district is facing a crisis or not."

As Diane predicted, Rob couldn't help himself and stopped by the new office area for teachers. Since the shift in the high school structure changed last year, and the necessity of teacher office hours became paramount, Rob led the charge to create an open, physical space that encouraged interaction between learners and teachers. The area was now filled with bright, glass-encased communal cubicles that teachers and learners could sign out to use. There was also ample common space for small group discussions or team meetings.

The group entered the Innovation Lab, so Diane wrapped up her explanation of leadership philosophy so they could interact with the learners and teachers in the lab. After a quick break, the tour group had settled back in and Rob brought up the importance of non-negotiable value statements and value clarification.

NON-NEGOTIABLE VALUE STATEMENTS

"ONE OF THE sayings that helped guide our process through the crisis was a quote by John Maxwell, 'How you view things influences how you do things.' As mentioned earlier, our leadership team believed that we should not let a crisis go to waste, and it should be used to further our long-term goals for the school district. In the middle of the craziness of the situation, we wanted to keep what Napoleon Hill called a 'positive mental attitude.' At the end of the day, we thought the best way to accomplish this was to focus on three principles.

1. Stay true to yourself.
2. Stay true to your students.
3. Stay true to your staff.

We felt if we did these things, then keeping a positive mental attitude would be easier. Notice I did not say it would be easy! We can remember how difficult those times were. Still, our mantra helped focus us on our New Learning Ecosystem and remember that we wanted to become radically learner-centered."

Rob turns toward the wall to his left and gestures to draw the audience to a quote that is painted on the wall and continues, "You will see on the wall that we have a quote by Roy Disney, 'It's not hard to make decisions when you know what your values are.' Our district believes a crisis does two things. First, it exposes a leader's values—for good or ill. Second, a crisis exposes whether leaders even have a set of articulated values."

Rob paused for a second to make sure what he was about to say gets across to the audience. "I have heard a lot of people talk about a feeling of being 'lost' and 'things were moving too fast' when they think back on the COVID-19 crisis. Truthfully, I think all of us felt that way at times. In my experience, the most effective strategy for school leaders to help them through a crisis is to take time for themselves to do two things.

1. Create a non-negotiable value statement about learning.
2. Create a non-negotiable value statement about leadership.

A hand went up in the back of the room. It was a principal from a neighboring school district. "I hope you're not talking about values as in religious values or morality because I do not feel comfortable having those kinds of conversations with my staff!"

"I am so glad you bring that up," Rob answers. "Personal religious or moral values may color what an individual creates when writing their leadership and learning values. However, I go back to what John Dewey said in Education and Experience. We short-change ourselves if we start to get into 'either-or' arguments where one side of an argument is always right, and the other side is always wrong. In the world we live in, the answer always lies somewhere in between two extremes. The non-negotiable value statements for leadership and learning are meant to be a 'stake in the ground' to help center the leader and the organization they are leading. Of course, the leader will justify why they chose those value statements, but the goal is to have the courage to say, 'This is what I believe in at all times, even during a crisis.' Does that help you at all?"

"Somewhat, thank you," comes the answer from the back of the room.

"Your question actually leads me into the next thing I want to talk about. A crisis demands that there are bedrock values and principles that a leader lives by. When a leader is not aware of their learning and leadership values, it is like you are driving a bumper car in an amusement park. You are violently pushed, pulled, and jerked into hundreds of different directions with little control over where you are going. Taking the time to create non-negotiable value statements in learning and leadership does not prevent the violent 'bumps' that occur in a crisis—but it does give you power steering. This allows the school leader to keep moving forward in the direction that will help their learners, school, staff, and community."

Jane speaks up, "The magic of the values clarification process are the conversations that are created. I am excited to talk to you about how our leadership team and the building PAT teams created their value statements."

VALUE CLARIFICATION

"Our goal was not to make the process too difficult. Remember, we were in the middle of the COVID-19 crisis, no one was sure what was going to happen in the short-term, let alone the long-term. We understood that we were living in a VUCA world, and we had to act quickly. The process we are explaining may not be what is described in the Harvard Business Review when they talk about 'best practices' in strategic planning, but it worked well for us under the circumstances at the time. We believe that you can use the process, or your version of the process, to get similar results."

She continues, "The first thing we did was develop our leadership philosophy. As a leadership team, we had been studying leadership intensely for a few years. The crisis forced us to use all the information we had put in our heads to make our own customized leadership philosophy. In our case, the leadership framework that grounded our thinking was the Total Leaders framework by Chuck Schwahn and William Spady. It is important to note that this is what we chose because we felt it worked well for our team, our school district, our staff, and our community. Any leadership philosophy helps people gain a shared understanding of the world. We used the Total Leaders framework because we felt that it allowed us to easily incorporate everything else we had learned about leadership into one easy framework. We encourage you to create your own. We strongly believe the process we used can be adopted by anyone to create their own value statements, regardless of the leadership philosophy they have adopted."

The rest of the presentation seemed to go well. The Secretary asked several clarifying questions and the other guests followed suit for another fifteen minutes. The audience was attentive during the rest of the tour and everything seemed to go well. The entire leadership team took a collective sigh of relief as the Secretary of Education and her entourage left the building.

As people filed out of the school into their waiting vehicles, Rob called an impromptu leadership team meeting in the lobby of the high school.

"I always think it is worthwhile to do a quick review of our meeting and tour. So, how did you think it went?" asked Rob.

Diane chimed in, "I have noticed a little hang up every time we talk about our story, and that is when we talk about our leadership philosophy and how we created the value statements. I think people are fuzzy about what it means and how to do it."

"I can see that too," said Brett and Craig nodded.

"Well, let's put this topic on our next leadership team meeting agenda so we can talk about how to be more articulate in this area. The topic is so important that we want to get it right," Rob said, as they all walked through the doors together.

Rob got into his car and took a deep breath. Today was a great day to share their story, but the concerns the leadership team brought to his attention just a few minutes ago weighed on him. A leader that grounds themselves and their school in a leadership philosophy sets themselves and their school up for success. "How can we be more articulate about that?" Rob asks himself. He started the car and drove through the parking lot to the school exit. He passed the school's track and field complex and saw the community "walkers" taking advantage of the nice day by walking on the track. The fact that these people were on the track was a result of his—and the school district's —philosophy. The school district has received so much goodwill from the community for allowing them to walk on the track. "How can I do a better job of explaining the importance of a leadership philosophy?"

The next day the phone rang in Rob's office shortly after he arrived. It was the principal who sat in the back of the room and asked the question about values at the presentation yesterday.

"How can I help you?" Rob asks.

"Thank you for taking my call, Rob. My name is Kermit, and I am the middle school principal at the school district a few miles west from you," he says.

"Nice to meet you. Thanks again for the question yesterday. People get more from our presentations when good questions are asked. What's on your mind today?" asks Rob.

"I am really excited about helping our superintendent make the changes in our district that you talk about in your district. Our community and staff are primed for a change, but we are struggling with how to start the process. I know you say to start with the leadership philosophy. We have done a lot of work about the situation we face right now in the district and we need to know how to start the work on solidifying a leadership philosophy. So, how do we start?"

"Maybe the best way to help you understand the 'how' is to share with you our leadership philosophy and the questions we asked around it," begins Rob. "As I mentioned in the presentation, there can be an almost unlimited number of philosophies that you create for yourself and your team based on what you have learned from leadership theory, leadership books, practical experience, and the particularities of your school district. For example, I know people that have built their leadership philosophy around the work of Simon Sinek and 'the why' question. I know districts that have dug deep into the Toyota method. I even know school districts that base their leadership philosophy around the principles of design thinking. My point here is for you to take what makes sense to you and use it as a foundation for your philosophy. It does not have to be perfect. It will be messy. But it will be yours, and that is the most important part of the entire philosophy."

"We actually have done a lot of studying around Covey's work. We think that it makes a lot of sense for us."

"That's a great place to start. Do you have about fifteen minutes? I want to share with you our leadership framework as an example of how the framework leads to the value statements that are so important for school leaders," Rob says.

"Sure, let's go!" replies Kermit.

2 FOUNDATIONAL QUESTIONS TO CREATE A LEADERSHIP PHILOSOPHY

"OKAY, IN OUR case, as you know from the presentation yesterday, we chose the Total Leaders framework that was developed by Chuck Schwahn and Bill Spady. We believe that Total Leaders is a good foundation for the work we need to get done in the school district. But before I explain the specifics of the framework, I want you to be cautious."

Rob continues, "No matter what framework you develop, there are universal questions that you need to ask yourself about any philosophy you choose that will help you create value statements.

1. First, think of an exemplar leader for each part of your framework that you have encountered in your career. How did they embody leadership in your framework?
2. Second, think of a leader that did not exemplify characteristics in your framework. How did they not embody the characteristics of the framework?

These are important questions. In our case, we asked these questions for each domain in the Total Leaders framework. I urge you to ask these questions for each section and subsection of whatever framework you choose. Does that make sense?" Rob asks.

There is a pause on the phone that Rob interprets as slight confusion. "I'll be honest with you," Kermit says, "It is not clear to me why we need to place so much time and effort on something as theoretical as a philosophy."

"Harry Truman once said that 'not all readers are leaders, but all leaders are readers.' I believe the work we do is so important that education leaders must read and think deeply about their craft. The best way to do that is to read about leadership. You can read books, newsletters, blogs, or even listen to podcasts. The important part is that leaders are engaging in arguments and thoughts that stretch their thinking. Once you do that, and it sounds like you and your team have done this, then you must make sense of what you have read. The process of incorporating the 'theoretical' to fit into your 'reality' is where the leadership magic happens. Even if you only want to manage your system, you are getting paid to make that system the best functioning system there is, so you must learn about best management practices. At the time of the COVID-19 crisis, and continuing to today, all of us must take the VUCA world at face value. Our leadership reality during the COVID-9 crisis, and today, is volatile, uncertain, complex, and ambiguous. Navigating this reality implies having a leadership foundation.," Rob finishes.

"That actually helps," Kermit answers, "I always have to be reminded that we are living in a VUCA world, and the fluidity of our reality requires constant attention and adjustment."

Rob grins, "I really like what you just said. 'Attention' and 'adjustment' are two good ways of looking at how we need to approach our own leadership journey."

11 QUESTIONS TO CREATE YOUR LEADERSHIP PHILOSOPHY

ROB CONTINUES, "I want to explain the Total Leaders framework. There are five domains to the framework: Authentic leadership, Visionary leadership, Cultural leadership, Quality leadership, and Service leadership. We developed questions for each domain to help build value statements later in the process. The questions are not specific to our framework, we just placed the questions in certain domains. You can do the same for your philosophy.

I am going to quote from the book now, 'AUTHENTIC LEADERS are masters of personal meaning and purpose. There is nothing pretentious or artificial about them. Their essence is value-based and personally grounded.' Now we ask universal questions that can be adapted to any leadership philosophy you choose. They are:

1. What do you believe about learning? ("Who is it for, where does it happen, how will learners access it," are great starting point questions)
2. What do you believe about teaching? (What does great teaching look like? What is the role of a teacher, students, and community?)
3. What are your non-negotiable beliefs about education? (Education is the system in which learning occurs. What are the assumptions you hold that make a great education?)
4. Why did you get into the teaching profession?"

Rob pause at this point to make sure he hasn't lost Kermit. At the end of the day, if someone only asked these four simple questions of themselves and their leadership team, they would gain clarity immediately and begin to make beneficial changes. These four questions served as the foundation for the work the school district did during the COVID-19 crisis. When it began, there was not a lot of time or budget to have a retreat or hire a consultant to work with him and the team, so they just started answering these questions for themselves and of each other.

"I'm with you, brother," Kermit says, "Keep going."

"The next domain is VISIONARY LEADERSHIP. Again, I will quote from the Total Leaders book, 'The essence of visionary leaders is paradigm-breaking imagination and innovation. They excel at creating novel possibilities that others don't see; chart new directions for their organizations and thrive on translating shifts and trends into productive options for organizational transformation.' There are three questions we aligned to this domain, although you can use the questions however you want for your leadership philosophy. Add these to the first four questions I asked you.

5. What is the next thing you need to know to excel at what you do? Why? This question is so important in the times of

COVID-19 because everything that we assumed about schooling and education has been turned upside down.

6. What skills do you need to develop?
7. What are you reading and what have you learned that applies to your school or school district?'

The third domain is CULTURAL LEADERSHIP. Quoting from the book, 'Cultural leaders shape the orientations, quality, cohesiveness, and energy of their organization's culture… Cultural leaders bring the value and purpose dimensions of authentic leadership to life in a direct, interpersonal way.' Our team created two questions for this domain. Add these to your list.

8. How do you create meaning for your staff in school? Specifically, how can you recreate meaning for your staff based on their new work reality?
9. How do you communicate your vision for education with staff, parents, students and your superiors?"

He paused and Kermit spoke up. "I see from your first question under culture how important it is to have your own leadership philosophy and value statements. I never thought about helping other people make meaning of the world and the direction of the school. I think of some of our faculty members who push back on things we ask them to do…maybe they just don't have the context of the situation and why we are asking them to change their practice. 'Do it because I said so' is not a viable answer when they ask you 'why.' We can head off some of the 'why' questions when we help make meaning for them."

"That's it!" Rob smiled. "That is a great insight into the power of a leadership philosophy."

"I want to continue with the fourth domain of the framework, QUALITY LEADERSHIP. I hate to be a 'quote' machine," Rob says, "but the authors do such a great job explaining the domains that I can't really add much. From the book, 'Change is productive when it involves more effective ways of operating and leads to consistently improved outcomes. The knowledge, skills, strategies, standards, and expectations that it takes to achieve these improvements is the domain of the quality leader.' The one question our team felt fit best in this section was this:

10. Describe your feedback loops that keep you up to date on your school's performance now that you are working in a virtual/ hybrid setting.

You may want to adjust this question somewhat since we put 'working in a virtual setting' at the end because of the situation with COVID-19, but you get the picture."

"Now you're cooking with gas!' Kermit exclaimed. "While reading Covey, we have talked a lot about feedback loops and how to make sure they become part of the system of our school!"

"So, you also know how difficult it can be to implement those systems of feedback loops. Feedback loops were the one area our team struggled with during the crisis and still struggle with today. Receiving honest feedback, and more importantly, being willing to hear honest feedback is hard work!" Rob inwardly cringed as he recalls how he personally had to "grow" in this area of listening to honest feedback.

"The final domain in our framework is SERVICE LEADERSHIP. 'Service leaders do everything possible to establish organizational support... They are committed to ensuring that their organizations are structured and aligned to achieve the declared purpose and vision.' We thought the question for this domain was time specific to the COVID-19 crisis. We didn't anticipate the question staying relevant beyond the crisis, but it certainly has.

11. How can you be a better example for your staff as they adjust to a new work environment?"

We used the context of the school closings to frame these questions. You can easily adjust this question by substituting a 'new work environment' for whatever change you are trying in your school or school district."

Rob took a breath. "I know this is a lot to take in, but has this been helpful?"

Kermit chuckled. "Absolutely! I think our district is doing a lot of the work you describe, but we don't have a name for it and didn't know how to recognize it for what it is. Whether you call it a leadership 'philosophy' or 'framework,' it's just a matter of reflecting on what we know about leadership from studying, and what we know about our unique school, staff, and community. I now see how tightly coupled the value statements are to the leadership philosophy because the questions are linked to it."

"Right on," Rob answers. "I hate to leave you at this important part, but our Board President is on the other line and wants to talk. Are you up for breakfast to finish this conversation? My treat. How about meeting at Butch's Café tomorrow at 9:00AM?"

"I'll see you there," Kermit replied. "I'll try to think of more questions between now and then."

CREATING YOUR VALUE STATEMENTS—A 4 STEP PROCESS

As KERMIT WALKS into the café the next day, he reaches into his pocket and feels the folded piece of paper that is there. He made sure he wrote down some questions that popped up after his conversation yesterday with Rob. Kermit didn't want to forget them. He sees Rob at a corner booth and slides in across from him.

Rob looks up from his phone and smiles. "What's happening? I can't believe you still decided to join me after my lengthy lecture yesterday," he joked.

"I am actually looking forward to starting the process of changing the structures in my school district," Kermit replied. "But first, what's the best thing on the menu?"

"Today's special is the Western Omelet—you won't be sorry you ordered it," says Rob. "Make sure you ask for extra salsa."

The waiter comes over and takes their order leaving Rob and Kermit time to talk.

"I thought about what you shared with me yesterday," Kermit began, "and I realize now how the questions you listed can be used no matter what your leadership philosophy is. They are truly universal. What interests me right now is how to use the answers to those questions. In other words, how do those questions lead to the two value statements for leadership and learning?"

> ## My Two Cents
>
> Remember, the most important part of the 4-step process is the conversation it produces.

"Let's dive right into that. My team uses a four-step process to deconstruct the answers to those questions and turn them into value statements. The same steps are used for each value statement. Once the value statements are created, the last step is essential, and we will get into that more after I explain the steps that lead to a value statement."

Kermit interrupts Rob at this point, "Is this 'process' that you talk about requires the school district to hire an outside consultant to come and facilitate the whole thing? Or is this something that can be done internally by those of us in the district already?"

"I always tell people that this is not rocket science, Kermit. The 'magic' in the process is the importance of starting conversations with key people in your district around leadership and learning. I believe there is great value in creating the statements, and they were essential for our district as we navigated the COVID-19 crisis. But even if you do nothing with the value statements, the fact that you talked about what people value in leadership and learning will benefit the schools and learners."

"That's a relief to hear," responded Kermit, "My superintendent is worried about the price of consultants, so she will be glad to hear that they aren't necessary for this particular process."

"Not necessary and I also believe you could find consultants that are reasonably priced if you wanted to go down that route," answered Rob. "It's a matter of knowing if you need the help or if you're on the path to figuring the answers out for yourself. So, let's talk about the four-step process to make sense of those eleven questions." Rob turns over the placemat in front of him, takes out a pen and starts writing.

STEP #1

"REVIEW YOUR ANSWERS to the first four questions I shared with you yesterday. What are the common themes—or words—that crop up? Think of stories from your career that exemplify your answers. Is there a student that comes to mind or a mentor that helped you? Write down those stories. Also, think of a colleague who did not exhibit the traits you describe in your answer. What were the outcomes for learners because of this? Do this for each one of the four questions. Write a one or two paragraph synopsis of your answers."

Kermit seems their food coming and hurries to ask for clarification before they get distracted. "Explain to me why we should think of people who are the opposite of what we think is the best. That seems like a potential waste of time."

"Simple, Kermit. Let me tell you a story. When I was a young teacher, I had a student in my American Government class who was a challenge. You know the kind: he was not mean spirited, but he was a 'handful.' Through lots of hard work on his part and mine, we got him through the class. Ironically, five years later, he landed a job as a custodian in the school. I was still a teacher, and one day he was walking by my room while I was teaching American Government and I asked him to step into the class. He gladly came into the room. He was a 'ham,' and I asked him to recite part of the Declaration of Independence. One of the assignments I always gave was to memorize the first third of the Declaration of Independence. He did it well, even after five years, and as he was walking out the door he said this to the class, 'I am a good example of a bad example, so learn from people who make mistakes!' That was great advice 25 years ago and is great advice today!"

"Good point," Kermit concedes, as he starts to butter his toast.

As the pair eat, Rob continues to write on the placemat and talk about the next steps in the process.

STEP #2

"SIMPLIFY IT. TAKE your one-paragraph synopsis and turn it into a 140-character Tweet. If you have a Twitter account, tweet it live! See what the reaction is. This forces you to condense and focus your ideas. The goal for a value statement is to make sure it reflects the essence of who you are as a leader and what you believe about learning. The goal here is the fewer words, the better. But do understand the distillation process is hard work. Mark Twain supposedly said, 'I apologize for such a long letter, I didn't have time to write a shorter one,' and that catches the crux of the work. Fewer words mean more clarity on the part of the person writing."

STEP #3

"IN THIS STEP, take your tweet of 140 characters and turn it into a subject line in an email. The ground rules here are that the subject should be less than 10 words and appeal both emotionally and practically to a reader—essentially, does it make someone want to open the email or send it to their spam folder? For example, I know a principal who created one that said, 'All kids can if all adults will.' Subject lines in emails, by definition, must be catchy and get the point across about what is in the email. It will be a challenge to go from 140 characters to less than ten words, but the intellectual sweat will be worth it, I promise."

"Do you actually make people do this on paper?" asks Kermit.

"Not only do they put it on paper," Rob answers, "I have them share out in large and small groups what they have written. Remember when I said the 'magic' is in the conversations? I have seen leadership teams learn so much about each other and actually grow closer together as they discover things about their colleagues that they just did not know before."

STEP #4

"NOW, CREATE A non-negotiable learning value statement based on your subject line. The statement can be no longer than one sentence and does not have to be a complete sentence. Write your completed non-negotiable value statement about learning. Some examples are, 'All students, every day, every way,' or 'Students first,' or 'What is the best interest of the children?' When someone is asked about their value statement for learning, they should be able to immediately recall stories and examples explaining why it is important for them."

Rob finishes his omelet and continues, "You use the same process to create the leadership value statements, using the answers from questions five through eleven."

MAKE THE VALUE STATEMENTS ACTIONABLE

ROB SIGNALED TO the waiter for the bill. "An important step in the process is what comes next, and that is to make your value statements actionable. There is no sense doing the tough mental work that you just put yourself through and then let it sit on a shelf somewhere! Leadership in a crisis is about giving traction in a world where there is a lot of distraction. I believe a big part of offering traction is helping the people around you with context. Context brings meaning to actions. Your value statements will be the traction for your staff, students, and school community. Our team has a lot of success communicating our values and what they mean for the school, staff, and students, regardless if we are in crisis mode or not. This is just what we do."

"Thank you for breakfast," Kermit said, as Rob settled the bill with their waiter.

"No problem," replied Rob with a wink. "Just make sure you do everything that we have talked about over the past two days and this will be the best investment I've ever made! Seriously, while we wait for the waiter, I want to tell you what our leadership team did to communicate our value statements to the school community. It is all based on a five-slide presentation. This is simple but incredibly effective.

1. On the first slide, state your non-negotiable value statement for learning.
2. On the second slide, state your non-negotiable value statement for leadership.
3. The third slide will demonstrate how these values will impact the work of your staff. What will you expect from them because of your values?
4. On slide number four, share with the staff how the value statements will impact your work. What behavior changes will they see from you because of the value statements?
5. In the final slide, share with the staff how your non-negotiable value statements will impact learners. How will learners, their parents, and the community know you are 'living' these values?"

"That seems doable," Kermit said as he finished his coffee. "It forces you to make what you have done actionable. I feel one of the criticisms of leaders, or at least poor leaders, is that they talk a lot but don't back up their talk with actions. Creating a short presentation forces a leader into the action step".

Rob slides out of the booth and laughs, tucking a tip under his saucer, "If I can manage to get out of this booth without pulling a muscle, I'll leave you with one more thing to think about.

Use the presentation as a foundation. You can expand and change the presentation depending on the audience you are speaking to. Reorder the slides, add other slides, create your own graphics. The important thing is to use the presentation to share what you believe about learning and leadership."

Walking through the door on their way to the parking lot, Kermit thanks Rob for his time and for sharing what he learned about leading an organization during the COVID-19 crisis.

Rob is happy that he spent the time talking to Kermit because he believes Kermit is ready to lead change in his school. He hopes that a significant crisis like the COVID-19 crisis does not happen again, but he also knows that the process he just explained to Kermit will help him through normal times as well.

BOOK STUDY QUESTIONS FOR CHAPTER 3

1. Do you have a well-articulated leadership vision for yourself? Do you have a positive, future-focused vision for your organization? If not, create one right now! When this is articulated, decision-making about all leadership questions becomes clearer—not necessarily easier, but clearer.
2. What do you want your learners to know, be able to do, and be like in the future?
3. Are you just reacting to a situation, or are you finding a way to leverage a situation to help reach your goal?
4. Are you intentionally designing a plan that will help you lead your organization to a better future? Where do you want to go and how are you going to get there?

5. What decisions that you used to think were important and urgent can now be classified as distractions? (Quadrant #4)
6. List some items that are unique to our current crisis that are not important but urgent. (Quadrant #3)
7. Everything cannot be a crisis. Based on your value statements and the goals for your school, what is important and urgent that belongs in Quadrant #1? Of these identified issues, which ones can be shifted into Quadrant #2?
8. What are the areas of alignment between your value statements and the goals for the school? What decisions do you face right now that will help you live your values and achieve the goals for the schools? Write these down and place them in Quadrant #2

BOOKS

1. The 7 Habits of Highly Effective People by Stephen R. Covey
2. Total Leaders by Charles Schwahn and William Spady
3. One Piece of Paper: The Simple Approach to Powerful, Personal Leadership by Mike Figliuolo
4. Start With Why: How Great Leaders Inspire Everyone to Take Action by Simon Sinek
5. To Sell is Human: The Surprising Truth About Moving Others by Daniel Pink

WEB SITES

1. Simon Sinek's web page is full of great information *https://simonsinek.com*

STAY TRUE TO YOUR STAFF

LEADERSHIP, SHARED VISION, SKILLS

"Everything is hard before it is easy."

—JOHANN WOLFGANG VON GOETHE

CHAPTER 4 CONCEPTS AND THINK-ABOUTS

1. Crisis Management Matrix
2. Empowering ALL staff
3. Your spheres of influence
4. Long-term and short-term gain in the professional development of staff

Driving away from the diner, Rob notices the time. "Shucks," he thinks. He is going to be about five minutes late for the meeting with the architects. The school district is undergoing a significant renovation in all its buildings. The new educational structures they have put in place in the school district require new physical structures of the schools. The biggest change is having fewer traditional classrooms and more versatile meeting spaces to accommodate learner-centered education. He's looking forward to the result of the project but knows any building project comes with high levels of stress—a stress he knows well from months of living with an unfinished first floor of his house during the pandemic.

Rob recognizes the feeling of excitement when thinking of the positive result of the building project and the anxiety of thinking about the process that will get the school there. It reminds him of the last time he had these two emotions coursing through him at the same time at work.

It was a presentation he did for his leadership staff not too long after his infamous "red-winged blackbird" walk. Rob wanted to emphasize to his leadership team the critical role the staff was going to play to help them through the COVID-19 crisis. He knew empowering the staff would take a lot of work—which made him anxious—but the outcome would be great for the staff, students, and the school. The team embraced empowerment intellectually when they introduced The New Learning Ecosystem before the crisis. However, he knew the crisis was going to force the intellectual understanding to a reality on the ground.

He stops at a traffic signal and thinks back to the day he made the "pitch" to his leadership team to stay true to the staff...

"Okay, everyone, let's have a seat," Rob said as he walked into the conference room.

He looked around the room and noticed signs of stress on everyone's face. The school district's buildings had been closed for three weeks. There was no "new normal" settling in yet. People felt unmoored. The school had just ramped up its online options to their learners. They purchased course content, and the teachers were using it with the learners to approximate the instructional experience of three weeks ago. Rob knew that the team was aware of their new leadership reality. They had intellectualized the VUCA world and how to respond, and they were passionately committed to The New Learning Ecosystem. The final piece of the puzzle was for Rob to stay true to the staff. In the VUCA world they were living in, this simply meant empowering the staff. Rob found a chart explaining the change process. He adopted the chart for schools and education and believed it will serve as a cornerstone on how to stay true to the staff.

"How's everyone doing today?" The team knew Rob always meant it when he asked the question and didn't want to hear a vague "okay" or "great."

"I am on the verge of feeling overwhelmed," answered Craig. "We have the lunch program working well. The devices are in the students' hands so they can do the instructional work we expect from them. We have a solid plan for getting instruction to those kids that don't have internet access. So, I feel good about those things. The part that makes me feel overwhelmed is the concern about instruction. Are we doing all we can to make sure all learners are getting top-notch instruction? This is what is keeping me up at night." Craig finished with a sigh.

Diane stops anxiously nibbling on a pen cap and chimed in. "I know where you're coming from Craig. Just this morning, I had four parent phone calls about our new school reality. These parents want us to do more or even expect more from our learners. I worry that we are doing an injustice to our learners right now."

"I understand," Jane answered. "But let's remember how far we have come and celebrate the successes along the journey to this point. Then we can think about our next steps. I've felt overwhelmed myself over the past three weeks. The last week is when I have really noticed it. During the first two weeks of the school closure, there were so many things that we had to do that were immediate concerns, that I didn't even have time to feel overwhelmed. I feel like this past week, something in my mind shifted from 'emergency' mode to 'long-term' planning mode. I think this shift is what is causing me stress. I now am looking into the future and this mindset changes the priorities for my work away from immediate concerns to focus it on our New Learning Ecosystem. I have to stop and look back at all that we have accomplished in the last three weeks to keep from feeling like we're drowning. This allows me to look at the future with a more positive outlook."

Natalie spoke up, which was a surprise because she tended to speak last during meetings. "It seems to me Jane has a great point. I really like the framework of a mindset change. We have gone from 'hair on fire' concerns to one of 'The New learning Ecosystem' concerns. Let's recognize the mindset shift, even celebrate it, and figure out what we need to do to make sure we are staying true to our long-term vision for the school district."

"I am up for the challenge," said Craig. "I'm just trying to think about where exactly to start taking actions in this VUCA world that will help us toward our long-term goals for the school district."

Rob was silent and pensive during the conversation. The team brought up some powerful points. The change of mindset concept was one that resonated with him. He was feeling just as overwhelmed as the team and anxious to find a way to honor that feeling while keeping everyone motivated. "Let's identify the problem we are trying to solve and then work on a solution," he offered.

"Let me take a stab at it since I started this whole conversation today," Craig replied. "The reason I feel overwhelmed is that I just can't see how

I can fulfill the promise of The New Learning Ecosystem within the reality of the education environment we are working in today. As I say this out loud, I suddenly realize it sounds incredibly egotistical to think I am the one that has all of the answers to solve this problem." Craig sketched a stick figure with a frown on its face on a piece of paper and wrote under it, "Ego Man" and shared it with the team. "I guess I am letting my ego creep into my thinking."

Diane laughed and said, "Don't beat yourself up, Craig. My take on working in a VUCA world is that we tend to want to provide certainty so much that we forget that all of us have a team that we can rely on. Leadership is about more than having the right answer or being the 'all-knowing' guru all the time. Your comments have caused me to reflect on the value of the teams we lead. We have spent a lot of time and effort making sure our staff is simply outstanding in every way. I have a sense they have great ideas that will be able to help us figure out the long-term issues we are now seeing come to light."

Jane spoke up. "To answer Rob's question, maybe the problem statement is, 'How can we make sure our entire staff is able to contribute to continuing our progress on The New Learning Ecosystem during these trying times?'"

"I love it," said Rob.

The entire leadership team engaged in the conversation. It took guts on the part of Craig to be the first to admit that he was feeling overwhelmed, but Jane's "mindset framework" resonated with the team and pulled them out of their collective anxieties.

Jane looked around the table. "The COVID-19 crisis strips away the 'non-essential' in our system of education. When school buildings are closed, the work of education becomes incredibly focused. This question has always been a part of our decision-making process. Unfortunately, during normal times the question competed for intellectual space with other 'schooling' questions. The system of schooling pre-COVID-19 required that other interests competed with the question of how to educate kids. Managing the system to make sure the busses ran on time, the curriculum was up to date, and other assorted 'managing' tasks often overshadowed the most important question of them all."

"It's almost quaint to look back over decisions that we thought were so important just three weeks ago," said Natalie. "The COVID-19 crisis has focused us; I just want to make sure we don't allow that focus to detract from our long-term goals. Over

> ## MY TWO CENTS
>
> Always stay focused on the long-term mission and goals of the school. In good times and bad, this focus is essential.

the last few years, all of us have spent political capital talking about The New Learning Ecosystem and why it is important for our students. We have trained staff on tools that will help them contribute to it. We have held meetings with important members of our community about how it will help the community. We need to make sure we don't throw that all away."

"I agree," Jane said. "I think the opportunity that presents itself in the post-COVID-19 world is that school leaders can retake the narrative of what education and schooling should be. Let's look at what we have done as a team so far. We have worked on our value statements for learning and leadership. We have shared these value statements with important people within our school system. Now is the time to restructure education based on what educators in the field know to be best. No longer should we have to wait for a policymaker or some partisan hack from some think tank in Washington to tell us how education should be run. Our focus for the long-term is now becoming learner-centered. Let's have the courage to pursue that goal with vigor and conviction. Rob, do you want to share your 'crisis leadership matrix' with all of us now? I've seen drafts of it and think it fits nicely into the conversation we are having."

SIX PRINCIPLES OF CRISIS LEADERSHIP

ROB FUMBLED WITH some computer cords and hooked his computer up to the projector. The screen displayed his "crisis leadership matrix."

Rob spent a lot of time researching how to lead change since the COVID-19 crisis started. Managing change in the pre-COVID-19 world was important, but often not urgent. As Jane mentioned earlier, there were so many other items that vied for the attention of the leadership team, that the conversations about change management did not take priority. This, or any crisis, makes the management of change an essential skill, not just to "get by" but to also use the crisis to help further the long-term goals of the school district. The saying "Don't waste a crisis" comes to mind. Rob adapted various change management charts and adjusted them to be relevant for education during a crisis. He was proud of the result and hoped it makes sense to the team.

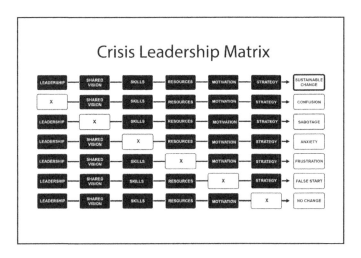

"I have taken ideas from other organizations and created the chart that is now projected on the wall," Rob began. "To make the most sense of it, look at the top row. There are six conditions that we must be aware of to make a lasting change: leadership, shared vision, skills, resources, motivation, and strategy. As you review the chart, notice that the column on the far right explains what happens if you are missing any particular piece. For example, if you do not have solid leadership, your staff, and system, will experience confusion. If you don't have a shared vision, you will experience sabotage within the system. I'll give you a minute to look through the chart and give you an opportunity to ask questions or give some feedback."

Rob waited as the leadership team reviewed the chart. As he looked at it for what seems like the thousandth time, the thought occurred to him: leadership comes from all levels of the organization. The discussion today drove the point home that everyone on the staff must get involved to help reach the goals of the school district. He made a mental note to himself to mention that to the team.

Diane started the conversation. "I like how the chart simplifies considerations to make change 'stick.' I also see the incredible amount of work that goes into each of the six conditions...to be successful at change management takes a lot of work. I also feel confident that we have done a lot of this work before the current crisis hit. For example, I think we've done a lot of work on strategy and shared

> ### MY TWO CENTS
>
> Leadership in a school comes from all levels of the organization. Teachers, support staff, and administrators all have potential to be leaders. To limit your leadership lens to just those in positional power is shortsighted. There are dedicated, passionate people throughout your school system...utilize their knowledge, skills, and passion.

vision. This bodes well for us as we move forward during this crisis time, I would think."

"I see that during these extraordinary times of living in a VUCA world, it is important to reexamine each of the conditions and ask ourselves 'what do these mean for our current situation?'" Jane added.

Craig looked up from his notepad where he was taking notes, "Reexamine is good, but we have to be careful not to throw the baby out with the bathwater. What are the fundamentals of each condition that help guide our work regardless of the situation? I think that's an important question."

Brett spoke up for the first time in the meeting. "The questions you are asking are the types of questions that were asked a lot when I worked in business before I came to the school district. I learned from my experience that it is important to review the conditions under the lens of the current situation in which we find ourselves. This is not the time for us to reconsider the work we have done. That would be foolish. Rather, we need to build from the work we have already completed during this crisis. What we have to concentrate on is to look at the conditions and make sure we are adapting the current leadership reality to them."

"Thank you, Brett, for grounding us in what is important," Rob said. "We have to remember that although we are living in extraordinary times, there have been times in history that have been just as disruptive. We can draw on lessons from these past times and learn from them. The bottom line is that we will come through this as a team and a school system. The way I view it, we have two choices. We can just sit back and let 'history' happen to us, and when we get to the other side, try to deal with the reality then. The other option is to 'change the arc of history' and influence what the world will look like when we come out on the other side of this crisis. Keeping our eyes wide-open to the possibilities and the opportunities presented by the crisis, while at the same time being realistic about the limitations inherent in the crisis is important."

PRINCIPLE #1 LEADERSHIP

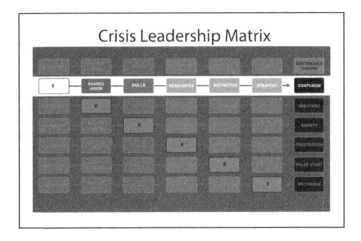

Rob noticed as he was talking that Jane was writing. "Jane, I see something inspired you. What are you thinking?"

"Well...this is not a complete thought yet. As we have been talking, I keep going back to the idea of leadership as it relates to your crisis leadership matrix. Our conversation started today with all of us sharing that we are feeling overwhelmed. Reading between the lines, I think we feel that we want to make sure all of our learners are getting the best education possible, and we believe we are reaching the limits of what we can do personally to make sure that happens. When I feel like that, I know I have to get other people involved. We have spent so much time developing our staff, so let's really double down and truly empower them. After all, leadership in this school district does not just sit around this table. We have leaders at every level of our organization, and we need to make sure we are capturing their passion, knowledge, and skills. In other words, everyone must help toward reaching our New Learning Ecosystem goals during the crisis."

Craig, who was sitting next to Jane, said, "Jane, I've been looking at the chart you made. I think you should share it with everyone. I don't know the specifics, but I really like the visual."

"Okay, but this is just a sketch," replied Jane. "I am not completely satisfied with my thinking on this yet, so I will appreciate your feedback."

SKILL/PURPOSE MATRIX

SHE TURNED HER notebook so everyone could see what she has drawn. "I keep going back to the fact that leadership is more than a position. Rob's chart reflects what the staff wants to see from leaders throughout the school—regardless if they are teachers or administrators. Every organization has positions of leadership. No matter the size of the organization, there is a group of people or a team that helps set the direction of the organization and strategizes tactics to help the organization perform well."

"Often," Jane continued, "people who find themselves in leadership positions got there because of the skills they learned and mastered in previous positions within the organization. Most of us sitting at this table are examples of the phenomenon of 'coming up through the ranks.' Waking up one day to find that you have moved from a job in which your skills and expertise centered on achieving a discreet task to one of leading the organization can be a jarring experience. Taking time to reflect on your new circumstances is essential. I think the matrix will help people clarify their thoughts when they are thinking about any position of leadership."

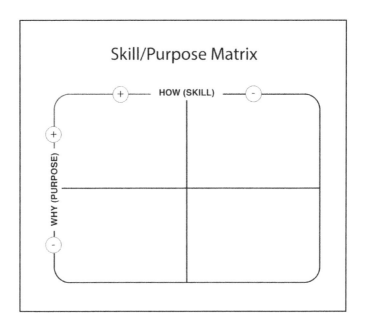

"Quick question Jane," Rob asked as he leaned forward to get a better look at the words on her chart. "Why did you choose 'purpose' and 'skill?'"

Jane flipped through her notebook and stopped to show the team a page with the header, Leadership Values. "Remember these? Creating our own leadership values started my journey of becoming a better leader. I believe we start with a leader's 'why' or 'purpose' because that's their foundation. We just went through the process of creating our leadership values. The process of creating my own leadership value statement was a real eye-opener. Once I had the statement completed, I felt a sense of calm about everything happening in our VUCA world. Did anyone else have a similar experience?" she asked.

"I don't know if 'calm' is the right word to describe what I felt after making my leadership value statement," Diane offered. "I was pretty far from 'calm!' The word I use is 'clarity.' I have a sense of clarity about what I professionally feel is best for education in general, and our school district specifically."

Craig raised his hand, like the good compliant student he was in school, and comments, "I can see where I did have some clarity and did experience some calmness. Although calm is a relative term these days. What I noticed after completing my leadership value statement was a sense of urgency. The fact that we have so much more to do for our learners and we cannot waste any time getting to where we need to go. I also don't want to waste this opportunity of the crisis to nudge things along a little quicker."

"That's great," Jane said. "I think too many leaders lose track of the reason they started in their career. Reconnecting to their deep, professional purpose creates a focused, decision-making lens."

"Let's move on to the 'how.'" Jane continued. "The 'how' are the skills that you need to accomplish your leadership value statement. Taking the time to create a list of skills that you need to help you reach your purpose is not so easy. The skills you need to accomplish your goals are constantly changing.... just think about how COVID-19 changed our skillset overnight after the Governor closed all school buildings. A skill-set that helps you with one project or situation may be helpful in the next situation, but not enough to be completely effective. You're always evolving."

"I agree," Karen chimed in. "I never gave one thought of how to effectively run a virtual faculty meeting, let alone think about how to give meaningful feedback to a teacher in an online environment. These are all things that I've spent a lot of time thinking about over the past three weeks!"

"The crisis has quickened the pace of learning the new skills necessary to be effective, that's for sure," Rob added. "Can you share with us what each quadrant in your matrix represents?"

"Sure," Jane answered as she turns to a page in the notebook that is filled with more notes. "I brainstormed some possibilities of what can be in each quadrant. Just remember this is an early concept for now. It needs to be refined, so bear with me..."

"Let's start with Quadrant Four: a leader in this space has low purpose and low skills. Through no fault of their own, they may have been promoted beyond their ability and are floundering. There are also people in this space who have not taken the time to reflect. Often these people believe they have all the answers and generally refuse to listen to new ideas because they don't want to damage their ego. The best resource to help leaders and staff in this area is the work of Brené Brown and her framework of vulnerability. Unfortunately, many people in this space probably are not going to be effective leaders."

"I guess the people in this quadrant can be the most frustrating for us to deal with," Karen said. "However, I do feel sorry for them. I think we have to find out what is going on with people in this quadrant and see if there is anything that we can do to help them out."

"Absolutely," Rob answered. "In some ways, it's our moral imperative to help move the people to another quadrant or help them find another career where it will be easier for them to be successful. We also must remember the context of the world we live in right now. How does this chart help inform us for moving our schools during this crisis?"

"I'll take a stab at that," Natalie replied. "In our immediate need for action and movement toward our goals, we are hopeful that there aren't too many people in this quadrant. For those that are, we can't push them too hard or ask them to move too fast—they're not going to budge if we use force. Showing them examples of their colleagues doing the work we know will lead to our short and long-term goals is essential. It gives them an example to see and they can come to the right conclusion on their own terms. In regular times, there's a lot more we can and should do to help this group of people. In our current crisis situation, giving them examples, giving them perspective, and encouragement is the best tactic."

"Thank you for bringing the discussion back around to our current situation Natalie," said Rob. "Jane, what about quadrant number three?"

"Quadrant Three leaders have high skills, but low purpose. These are leaders and staff who need to connect with their deeper purpose so they can utilize their skills effectively. People in this space may not be aware that they hold the skills needed to accomplish their goals because their goals and purpose are not well defined. Helping these leaders and staff align their skills with their purpose helps them as individuals and helps the organization in which they serve."

"Jane, we discussed earlier how we cannot create the changes we want to make to become radically learners centered with just those of us in this room, especially under the current crisis. Do you see that this quadrant is where we can find people on our staff that are an 'untapped' resource?" Diane asked.

Karen spoke up before Jane could answer. "In my long experience in education, and I include myself in what I am about to say, it is easy for a teacher to become satisfied with the way things are. Every school year has a rhythm

SPHERE OF INFLUENCE

Sphere of Influence: The people and organizational systems that you can positively influence.

that is comfortable and soothing. Think about the flow of the year from the first day of school to the last day of school. If you string too many of these years together, you find yourself fifteen or twenty years into a career, and you wonder where the time went. Even more insidious, you forget your 'why.' That's why it's so important to have our entire staff complete their learning value statements. It will remind them of the reason they started teaching to begin with. It took a veteran administrator to talk to me about what I wanted for kids and my career to snap me out of the complacency I was in. I knew I was a good teacher, but I was not offering anything beyond teaching. I discovered that my sphere of influence was too small for comfort."

"Okay, so let's remember that Quadrant Three is a place we can find some untapped leaders in our school district. As we look forward to the next few weeks and we double down on our New Learning Ecosystem, it's important that we pay attention to staff that have the qualities Karen just mentioned," Rob suggested.

"I'll move on to the next quadrant, if you all don't mind," Jane said with a smile—everyone was quick to find real-world examples of her leadership quadrants, so she must be on to something useful! "Quadrant Two leaders have low skills and high

SYSTEMS THINKING

Systems Thinking: The web of interconnectedness that helps leaders understand how things unfold over time.

purpose. We have all seen leaders and staff in this quadrant. They are the passionate believers in a cause who mistakenly believe that the world will bend to their wishes because their purpose is so obvious and good. They forget that leadership is about influencing people and organizations, and the study of how to do this is important. I just read The Fifth Discipline by Peter Senge and systems-thinking is top of mind for me. People in this quadrant will benefit from professional development about systems-thinking and the power of influence. It is exciting to have an enthusiastic member of our team, but frustrating for them when they can't accomplish what they set out to do. Helping them build systems is a great way to start."

Jane pointed to her diagram and continued, "The final quadrant is Quadrant One, and it describes leaders who have high skills and high purpose. This quadrant is aspirational for most of us since we are always evolving our skills. However, most of us have had the pleasure of working with, or for, someone in this space. They are effective leaders who make leading look easy. You know you are with a great leader if they make their job look easy—when we know it's anything but simple."

COMPLIANCE VERSUS AGILITY

"Jane, I don't know if I have a question or just a random thought," Craig said, as he frowned at his own notes. "I just can't get a dichotomy out of my head as I listened to your really thorough explanation for the matrix you developed—it's great! But there's a tension in my job between 'leading' and 'managing.' The tension occurs when the skills and the why on your matrix don't intersect between leading and managing. Are the skills for each aspect unique, or do they align with each other? I know to become an effective leader you must be an effective manager. Striking a balance between leading and managing is essential—not only for those of us with the title 'principal' or 'superintendent' but for all of our staff. Think about it, a teacher with few management skills will struggle to be an effective instructor."

He paused, waiting for the group to absorb the tension he felt. "Go on, Craig," encouraged Rob. "I think you're on to something critical."

"Okay, the first step in embedding leadership into your school is to define the difference between leading and managing. This is not to imply that one is more, or less, important than the other. What I am saying is that it is important to dissect the differences and start to understand where you are on a leadership/manager continuum."

Everyone around the table knew Craig often struggled with the friction between leadership and management. A high school principal can easily allow themselves to become too heavily entrapped in either direction, toward leadership or management. It was a topic he often brought up at their team meetings as he sought clarity for his own career journey.

He continued, "All of us have a certain predisposition when it comes to where we feel comfortable in the leadership/management spheres. The important part is not where you land on the continuum. The importance is that you recognize your comfort zone. It is knowing that you tend to lean in one direction or the other keeps you from becoming biased in one or the other.

As I mentioned before, I am not putting a stake in the ground and claiming that leadership or management is more important than the other. What I've done in my mind is to create components of leadership and management. Two components continually come to mind when I think about this topic—and you all know I think about it a lot!

One component is agility. The other is compliance assurance. It seems to me there is a continuum of where leaders fall. Compliance is an important facet of our job. Making sure that State and Federal regulations are complied with is a moral and ethical requirement. Maybe even more so now. However, you can become too focused on compliance issues. The saying 'paralysis by analysis' comes to mind. Let's face it, anyone can become overwhelmed by the smorgasbord of compliance issues facing education leaders but trying to guarantee perfection in compliance of all programs leads to fear. Think of Ben, from our neighboring district."

Rob knew exactly what Craig meant by bringing Ben up as an example. "One of my most popular blog posts on our district web site was entitled 'Compliance Zombies,'" said Rob. "The point of the blog post was to warn leaders not to become too reliant on compliance issues as a measuring stick on whether or not you are doing a good job. I was also careful to state something similar in the blog to what you just said, Craig. Like it or not, compliance is an important part of our role as school leaders. It just has to be coupled with other measures of success."

"Remember how hard it is to come up with other measures of success," said Karen, as she reorganized the stack of notes in front of her. "I know all of us have started the conversation about alternate measures of success for the new leadership reality we are facing. I am finding it's difficult to get people beyond test scores. There are so many other ways to measure success. Still, our system of schooling from the Federal level to the State level glorifies and requires some sort of assessment criteria, which is a compliance issue we face every year."

"I can see where the word 'compliance' and test scores can get conflated," Rob said. "In a lot of ways, test scores are the ultimate compliance weapon, hanging over the heads of all educators like the sword of Damocles. But we must be careful not to have a knee-jerk reaction in education to bring everything back to test scores. In this instance, I think Craig is talking about setting a structure within a leader's purview that realistically sets standards of excellence. Obviously, part of the structure will have a component of test scores and what we build around that is up to us. I have a friend that says our job as leaders is to be 'creatively non-compliant,' meaning we should all go to the limits of what is required and create our own ways to measure whether we are successful or not."

"I get what you are saying Rob," replied Diane as she looked up from her notes. "The challenge lies in the fact that most of our teachers, administrators, and other leaders have been raised in the accountability/measurability/sanction system created in 2002 with No Child Left Behind. Many people simply do not know any other system other than a compliance system. What you're suggesting is completely unfamiliar territory."

Rob paused a moment before answering. He was always proud when someone on the leadership team disagreed or pushed back and he was keen to honor the act of "disagreeing with the boss."

"I have never really thought about it like that, Diane. It seems that the default answer for anything that smells of compliance in education is to talk about test scores. I get it and it's worth talking about. For now, let's get back to the continuum that Craig is talking about and see if we can help him sort through this dichotomy. On one end, there is compliance, and on the other end, there is agility. Craig, what did you mean by agility?"

"This is going to sound corny," Craig said. "But I wrote a slogan down to try to capture my feelings on this. Here it is: 'Agility in leadership is having the courage to speak when there is not an easy answer.' A lot of times, it is easy to fall back on a rule or policy to give you an answer...and sometimes it does. But we all know that in a VUCA world, there are many instances where there is no 'right' decision, only decisions that can have multiple outcomes. Courageously pivoting to make decisions based on limited knowledge in an uncertain world is my definition of agility.

> QUOTE
>
> Agility in leadership is having the courage to act when there is not an easy answer.

Think of a time when you had to change what you planned on doing. For example, you may have planned on doing staff evaluations, but you notice a grant opportunity that's due in a few days, so you immediately start planning for that by convening a grant workgroup. We all experience this in our daily lives. The trick is to take that same agility you exhibited 'on the run' and apply it to planning long-term. Seeing opportunities where others may see barriers helps your organization. It was musician Rita Coolidge who said, 'Too often, the opportunity knocks, but by the time you push back the chain, push back the bolt, unhook the two locks and shut off the burglar alarm, it's too late.' Being agile means you kick down the door and lead your organization into the future. Don't let the door to opportunity remain closed due to reliance on policies, rules, and procedures."

"That makes a lot of sense," said Karen. "I see what you mean about there is no right or wrong on the continuum, only that you can't live on either end too much and be too afraid to move forward and lead. I think we also agree that we should heavily lean towards the agile side."

The rest of the team all nodded in agreement.

Rob cleared his throat. "That's an excellent reminder to keep progressing. We can't let ourselves get stuck in the weeds—or we'll end up managing just this crisis while abandoning our goal to become learner-centered. We must stay focused on where we want to be and make decisions that will get us there. So, to piggy-back on this topic of continuums, I'd like to talk about how we can avoid getting mired by policy and remain agile."

FUTURE-CENTRIC VERSUS POLICY-CENTRIC

"THE NEXT CONTINUUM is Future-Centric versus Policy-Centric. Education, as an industry, is heavily monitored. The fact that taxpayer money is being used leads to a high level of scrutiny by politicians and the public. Education is also a human business. Students and staff are the reason for the existence of education institutions—and humans are 'messy.' They don't act as you think they should. They have their own agendas. They make crazy mistakes. For all these reasons, there is a plethora of written rules or policies to try to control the chaos."

Rob scanned the room to make sure he wasn't losing anyone. He continued, "Policies help leaders maintain control. Policies also bring a sense of continuity to organizations—people know upfront what the rules are and that establishes a path. Policies also signal to the outside world the priorities of the organization. Whether it is a policy on curriculum materials or chaperone behavior on field trips, policies are our attempt at control.

I once read somewhere that policies are, in most cases, reactive. They are reacting to something that jeopardized continuity or muddied that messaging to the outside world. In my first superintendency, the policy dealing with athletics was twenty-three pages long with three administrative regulations on top of that. Reading through the pages was like an archeology dig. You could almost picture the situation that made the

> ### MY TWO CENTS
>
> School leadership requires some reactive moments...after all, when you deal with people and systems, there are times when you must react. Effective school leaders make sure that they spend more time being proactive. Being proactive means scanning the education environment and deciding how to lead your school toward the established long-term goals and vision.

superintendent and Board develop that policy. Is that helpful for you Craig?" asked Rob.

"Yes," Craig answered. "I would add that the danger of concentrating too much on control and policy is the organization becomes stale. Policies are a reaction to influences in the outside world, whether they come from the State or Federal government or from the people inside the organization."

Craig rose from his chair more as an attempt to clear his thinking as to stretch. "Becoming proactive causes your organization to become future-focused. As leaders, we can do an environmental scan of the field of education. What are the innovative trends in curriculum, instruction, technology, and school structure that you can leverage for change in your school? There will always be a policy to help manage the school, our job is to couple the policy mindset with a future-focused mindset. When working in a VUCA world, the importance of making all of the staff aware of the importance of being future-focused is paramount." Craig sat back down in his chair and reached for his water bottle.

"That's a good call," answered Rob. "In relation to the crisis leadership matrix, leadership is about empowering staff and finding the leaders that will help us through the current crisis. If we are experiencing a sense of being overwhelmed in the next three weeks for the same reason we are today, then we have not looked hard enough for the staff that can work with us to lead us through the crisis."

PRINCIPLE #2 SHARED VISION

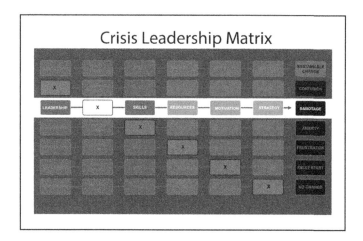

It was now Rob's turn to get up from his chair for a stretch. He walked over to the whiteboard but didn't make a move to write anything on it. He studied it for a moment before turning to face the leadership team. "In our VUCA, COVID-19 environment, a leader's job is to prevent as many distractions for people as possible. Notice I did not say 'eliminate' distractions...we know that's impossible and you can get bogged down if you even entertain that as a possibility. What we can do is create conditions for our staff and community that lessen the distractions. In essence, leaders need to do what John Maxwell suggests—offer traction in an uncertain world. Think about what we have experienced in the past three weeks. The disruption to our paradigms of education and schooling are remarkable and it's been hard for those of us in this room to digest the changes.

Imagine the disruption for your staff. We've spent countless hours over the past two years talking about change, innovation, and disruption in the context of our system and structures, and we still find ourselves without traction. Imagine our staff members who have not been so deeply involved in discussions of change and disruption. They've had all this chaos thrust upon them in a matter of days. You can see where they may feel adrift in our current situation."

"It is interesting you bring this up," Karen said. "I was talking to one of our teachers today, and she is doing a fabulous job transitioning from a brick and mortar teacher to an online teacher, and she said something interesting. She told me that she is actually really struggling with the whole situation. The stay at home order. The social distancing. Not physically seeing her learners. She said she just doesn't feel right. From my perspective, she's one of our best examples of a successful transition to online education and even she is struggling."

"I believe there has to be a certain level of unease in our current situation," answered Rob. "I understand that. Our job as leaders in this, or any crisis, is to make sure our staff is constantly reminded about our shared vision for the school, our learners, and our community. Although this may not eliminate the unease, it offers an anchor in these turbulent times. We are fortunate to have spent a lot of time in the past two years creating a shared vision...we just need to remind people of it and use it as a lens to make sense of what is happening in the world today."

Rob tapped a marker at the Crisis Leadership Matrix on the whiteboard. "Let's look closer at the matrix and see what happens when you don't have a shared vision. In times of crisis, the problem of a lack of shared vision is even greater. Without a shared vision, there will be

> ## QUOTE
>
> If your staff is unaware of the school district's vision, how can they know if their actions and attitudes are aligning to what the school is trying to accomplish?

sabotage within your organization. A small portion of the sabotage will be intentional, but most of it will be unintentional. If your staff is unaware of the school district's vision, how can they know if their actions and attitudes are aligning with what the school is trying to accomplish or unintentionally eroding the vision? Earlier, we discussed the importance of creating your own value statement for leadership and learning. We do this so people know our values and what we believe is important about educating learners. The added benefit is that we clarify for ourselves what is really important for our school, learners, and community."

Craig spoke up, "Ok, this is what resonates with me so far on this line of thought. I like when you said people may unintentionally sabotage the changes that the organization is trying to make. I believe that most of our staff will always do what is best for our learners. At times, we must do a better job of giving the context in which potential changes occur. In our case, right now, in our VUCA world, that means changes are thrust upon us and we must make these changes to reach our shared vision.

We are not talking about 'nice to haves' or the next cool, shiny program being offered by a vendor. The heart of the matter is simple. We are talking about change as a necessary process for the survival of our vision. With everything we have talked about so far today, I can see where unintentional sabotage can occur. If our staff unintentionally sabotages the changes our schools must make, that is on us. The responsibility of everyone sitting around this table is to make sure there is no unintentional sabotage. We all need to own the responsibility of not communicating our vision enough if it does happen."

Diane was eager to back Craig up. "Right on, Craig! Obviously creating your own vision is not enough: you have to nest that vision within the larger context of the school community. An elegant vision statement that just hangs on our office wall, or on the walls of the school, is meaningless unless we make sure it is used to offer traction for our staff, community, and learners. The most difficult part of a shared vision is making sure the 'shared' part is happening with the everyone outside of the leadership team."

MY TWO CENTS

The school's vision is the North Star of all you do as a leader. A great way to create meaning for everyone in the school system is to cascade the vision from the top of the organization to the bottom. Better than giving people the goals to reach, you offer them the meaning, or the reason, for the goals.

Rob was pleased to see the group speaking so passionately about communicating the vision. "Let me know what you think of this. We know what to expect from ourselves and those around us to make the vision happen. Now is the time to cascade our vision. Your staff knows our vision on a 30,000-foot view, but now is the time to make it more granular for them so that it can be applied to daily life and stay constant during a crisis. Remind them that our vision and goals have not changed for the school. As a matter of fact, in a VUCA world, vision is even more important. Over the past two years, you have met with your staff and done preliminary work on talking about their vision for learning. Now is the time to reconnect and have a conversation within the context of our current situation. How can their vision align with the larger vision of the school? Better yet how is their vision relevant to our current COVID-19 education setting?

I hope in this discovery process, you will find points of alignment and points of contention between their pre-and post-COVID-19 vision. It seems natural there will be changes in the 'how' of their vision. The important thing to remember is to cascade the shared vision from the community/school level to the level of the classroom teacher within the context of the crisis we face right now." Rob sat back down in his chair.

"What I am hearing so far," Jane stated, as she slid a bottle of water over to Rob's place, "is that to 'stay true to our staff,' the shared vision helps them keep at the top of their mind our eventual destination. The destination in our school is the New Learning Ecosystem and becoming radically learner-centered. The destination has not changed, only how we get there. Does that sound about right?"

PRINCIPLE #3 SKILLS

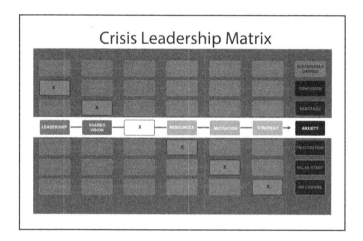

Natalie had been quietly listening to the conversation up to this point. "I think it does, Jane. I also want to take this idea of 'being true to our staff' one step further," she said. "I see on the chart that the next principle is called 'skills.' I'm not sure what you have in mind for this section Rob, but I have some thoughts about it."

"Go ahead," Rob answered. He pulled a loose sheet of paper from Jane's notepad and began making his own notes.

Natalie cleared her throat. "Okay, if people don't feel they have the requisite skills to accomplish what they are undertaking, then there will be large amounts of anxiety. In the pre-COVID-19 world, I had a hard time understanding leaders who expected their staff to undertake a new way of doing things without providing the necessary professional development for them. To me, it seemed like they were putting the cart before the horse. In our current crisis, skill acquisition for our staff is even more important than before. I like what Rob said about cascading the vision. Once we have the vision of the school cascaded into an articulate whole, we must make sure there is action to achieve the vision. More than action, we have to consciously think about the skills it will take to achieve the vision."

"I can certainly see that providing great instruction online is an important skill for our staff during this crisis," Karen said. "I think that all crises offer a chance to offer professional development to help achieve the vision of the organization. The first step in the process is to identify the skills our teachers will need to implement the change. What are the essential skills that teachers will need when interacting with learners in our new 'reality' to make sure our change works and is viable? Once these are identified, you simply provide the necessary training."

Brett looked up from his tablet. "I actually would like to add one more thing to that list: pay our teachers when they attend training. One of the most asinine things I hear in schools is that people expect teachers to do significant training without being paid. Come on! What other industry would tolerate that? If we want our vision to be implemented and we know that it is going to require time beyond the regular business hours for schools, then pay them for their time. I know I am the business manager, and I'm supposed to be the one you expect to be fiscally conservative, but really? I believe we should always pay teachers for their time in training, especially in this time of crisis, since it will help us reach our goal of becoming radically learner-centered."

Everyone chuckled at Brett's impassioned statement. All the people in the room are guilty of looking at Brett sheepishly at some point in the year when they want to spend money that is outside the ordinary budgeted items.

"You know," Karen stated, "You have probably heard of the 80-20 rule. It states that 80% of your success comes from 20% of your work. The same 80-20 principle applies to our staff when you think about who will lead us through this crisis and to help us become learner-centered. 20% of our staff will get us 80% of the way there. It seems reasonable that we will want to concentrate our efforts on that 20% when we initiate our training. It will probably be a good idea to include them in some of the preliminary discussions about what kind of training they need. After all, they have been in the trenches doing this work for three weeks. I have come to think of the staff as living in three categories: rock stars, karaoke stars, and no stars."

The meeting had been going on for a while by that point and it was clear people were starting to feel a little "punch drunk" from the mental exertion the conversation has required. A break was soon becoming a necessity.

"Karen, are you suggesting that we have a 'school districts got talent' event? A sing-off to identify the best singers?" joked Craig.

"No, I see more of a The Voice competition where the best singers receive a coach," answered Red. He seldom spoke at meetings, so his response got everyone's attention. A handful of them happened to know that Red was the most talented musician in the group and would win any talent competition among the leadership team.

"Hardy-Har-har," Karen said with a smile. "Seriously though, every staff, in every school, has these three types of people: rock stars that take off with little encouragement, karaoke stars that will do well and get the job done, but only after being shown the music and given the melody to sing, and no stars are those, for whatever reason, will not, or cannot, be moved to do what needs to be done for the organization. How we address these three categories of people will determine how successful we are at successfully navigating this crisis."

"I am dying to hear about these three categories," Rob said. "I think this is an important framework for us to consider as we think about moving forward and doubling down on our New Learning Ecosystem vision."

ROCK STARS

> ## MY TWO CENTS
>
> Call this group "rock stars" or what-
> ever you want, just make sure you
> find them and engage them. They
> will help lead any initiative that you
> have for the district and will be the
> leaders toward reaching the school's
> vision. You always engage all your
> staff in reaching the school district's
> vision, and this is the group you
> must engage with first.

"Let me get right into it then," Karen said. She worked her way to the whiteboard in front of the room. She wrote "Rock Stars" on the board.

"We would find rock stars in about 5-10% of our staff if I had to guess. They're rare and valuable. Rock stars can't wait to start something new. They get their energy and purpose at work from being out in front of the pack. In other contexts, they are called 'first adopters.' When considering how to implement our change, our first order of business is to get these people on board with how we want to move forward in the crisis. Here is how we can do that." She writes the following underneath Rock Stars.

1. MAKE THEM FEEL SPECIAL. "Rock stars want to be on stage, they want to be in the spotlight...let them!" Karen explained.
2. CONNECT THEIR PASSION TO OUR VISION OF THE NEW LEARNING ECOSYSTEM. "We have done a lot of hard work over the past three years on creating a vision, we just need to reconnect them to the vision in the context of this crisis. Help them make sense of our current world through the lens of our existing school vision," she continued.
3. LEAD EVERYONE. "It will take more than just having this 5-10 % of people doing the work," Karen said. "Therefore, we must help our rock stars spread the initiative they are undertaking. Make sure we give them the skills to articulate the reconnection of the school vision with their friends and colleagues on staff. Reinforce how their lives and those of

learners are better because of their work. Help them increase their zone of influence."

"Let's take five minutes to identify the rock stars on your staff. Make a list of those teachers, when you have completed your list, we will share our lists with each other. Remember, this is about 5-10% of your staff." Karen sat back down to sketch out her own list of rock stars.

She thought this would be a solitary undertaking with the leadership team, but apparently group work was the theme of the day. After compiling their list, the building principals couldn't wait to share the names with each other. Since most of the people sitting at the table had either worked with, supervised, or hired most of the teaching staff, everyone had an opinion on who qualified as a "rock star." The conversation was rich, with some adding people or subtracting staff from their original list.

KARAOKE STARS

"OKAY," KAREN BROKE in. She returned to the whiteboard and wrote "Karaoke Stars." "I see we have identified our rock stars. Let's put that list aside for a second and talk about karaoke stars. Karaoke stars make up about 70% of our staff. These are professional people who want to do well for learners but will not be the first people to try new things—they need a lot of encouragement. As a matter of fact, they will sit back and wait for other people to try new things before deciding whether they will participate. They are watching from the audience as the rock stars climb the stage for the first time. Karaoke stars hold the key to whether the changes we want to make in our school during the crisis will be successful or not. So how can we get karaoke stars on board? There are two things you can do to help this group." She wrote two statements underneath Karaoke Stars on the whiteboard and turned to explain them to the group.

1. SHOW THEM HOW IT WILL BENEFIT THEIR WORK.
   "Remember, karaoke stars are professional people who want to do well for learners. They are just not naturally inclined to be out in front of anything without support and examples of success. They must see that the changes they are experiencing

during this crisis will lead to a better outcome for their learners and themselves."

2. INCLUDE THEM IN THE WORK OF THE ROCK STARS. "Keeping in touch with them as we start to work with the rock stars is a must. We offer the context for the change taking place with the rock stars. In this way, misconceptions about what the rock stars are doing are lessened. The karaoke stars will eventually approach us and want to start the new work, and we can include them when they are ready. I suspect they will be ready sooner rather than later because of the acuteness of the current situation."

"Now, let's make a list of karaoke stars and add them to your list of rock stars. Remember, this will be about 85% of your staff."

Creating the list of karaoke stars does not take as long as the rock star list. The leaders sitting around the table were driven and figured out what their next task was going to be as Karen finished explaining how to help them. Feeling a little playful, Karen decides to "check for understanding" since the team seemed to make their list while she was talking.

She cleared her throat to get the group's attention. "So, who wants to answer this simple question: how can we lessen potential misconceptions with the karaoke stars as we work with the rock stars?"

"I know what you are doing," Craig answered, "and you are not going to 'get' me. I can multitask with the best of them! To answer your question, we must constantly communicate with the karaoke stars as we are starting our work with the rock stars."

Karen took a piece of candy from the communal candy jar on the table and tossed it to Craig, "Bingo!" she said. "Keep them involved."

NO STARS

"THE LAST GROUP is no stars," she began and wrote "No Stars" on the whiteboard. "No stars are those employees who will rail against anything new. I am not going to try to list all of the personal and professional reasons that there are 'no stars' in any school staff. What I am saying is that I believe they make up about 5% of the staff. I do not have a lot of patience for this group. They may be fine people outside of the school setting, but in the school, they interfere with change. The best and ethical way to approach this group is to explain our vision for the school, how the vision is helping learners, and our expectations for the changes they will have to make to implement the changes necessary to reach the vision. In most cases, we will get a minimum level of agreement from the no stars to do what they need to do.

The critical question we must answer is: What is the minimum level of engagement that we are willing to accept from this group? Once we answer that question, we can address the people that are failing to meet our minimum standard of behavior change. I suggest a 'come to Jesus' meeting where they leave knowing they need to switch schools or careers. What we do for the education of learners is too important to be ruined by people that do not want to help, especially during our current crisis. We may need to encourage them to leave the school system. Again, these may be good people, but that does not mask the fact that they are not good people RIGHT NOW for our school! We need to have the guts to have the tough conversation and get them on board or off the stage!"

After completing the final list of "no stars," the leadership team devised strategies to engage each group. The timelines for engagement and action was tight because of the current crisis situation. Rob was adamant the timelines must be aggressive. He, and the entire team, didn't want a "new normal" of not being learner-centered to creep into the organization. The conversation quickly turned to professional development planning for the group of "stars."

Rob began to tell one of his favorite stories to help get the group back focused on their task.

"On my first day of teaching 27 years ago, I entered the high school auditorium with 300 other teachers. I was expecting magic! I was pumped up to start my career and learn something new in the first three days before learners walked through the door. As I walked into the auditorium, I noticed something peculiar. The front half of the auditorium, the half

TEACHER EFFICACY

Teacher efficacy is when teachers believe their actions will help their learners.

closest to the stage, was empty while the very back rows were full of teachers. Hmmm, I thought. I wonder why people are sitting in the back? I quickly discovered that my idealistic anticipation of professional development was going to be sorely tested. Although some teachers listened to the onslaught of speakers for the entire day, most teachers were half-engaged, at best, and a good proportion were totally disengaged. Education has come a long way since then. Professional learning is no longer 'sit and get' but now includes job-embedded activities that respect teacher efficacy."

"Your story reminds me of my first in-service day too," Karen said. "I am glad we don't put our teachers through that anymore. I do, however, believe we have to think deeply about our professional development plans in light of the current situation".

While Karen and Rob were talking, Jane flipped through her notebook. When she found what she was looking for, she said, "I took notes at our professional development task force meeting last month. Actually, the meeting happened just two weeks before the school buildings were closed by the Governor. I really liked what we started to talk about at the meeting. We basically said that we can look at professional development through the lens of empowerment of teachers, and the impact of the training on the school system."

"What a relevant topic! I bet you didn't think you would be pulling out those notes for a while as you were trying to figure out our new leadership reality over the past few weeks," Rob said.

"You're right there, Rob," Jane replied, "but I am glad I thought of it as we were discussing characteristics of successful change. I want to share with all of you the definitions of empowerment and impact the task force produced, and then review the PD matrix the task force created.

- Empowerment is defined as: the sense that staff has autonomy in how they can go about their job to reach their own professional goals and the goals of the school district.
- Impact is defined as: the change in an organization because of the professional learning activity.

Here's a matrix to help conceptualize the relationship between empowerment and impact."

Jane displayed the matrix on the wall using the room's projector.

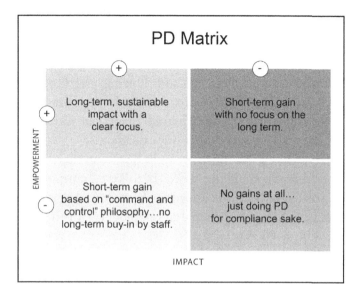

Jane continued, "We obviously are aiming to be in the upper left-hand corner of the matrix where there is high empowerment and high impact. It seems equally obvious that we want to empower our staff to make sure the impact is high. Let's dig into that assumption a little bit deeper. Empowering someone else means that we are giving some control to someone else. Are we comfortable with that?"

Natalie took a stab at answering the question, "I think we have to be honest with ourselves on this one. Giving up some semblance of control is difficult. Although we may intellectualize the fact that giving up control is good, it is difficult for most of us to do that. In most cases, we are sitting in these chairs because we are doers. We are problem solvers. We act. Consciously giving up control in some areas is necessary and a must in our current situation, but I want all of us to be mindful that it is not an easy thing to do."

> ## MY TWO CENTS
>
> Leaders must let go of their egos and give up some power and authority to reach meaningful, learner-centered goals.

"Thank you for taking the elephant in the room and slamming it on the table so we can face it," Rob said. "Giving up some control is hard, and we need to support each other through the process. As Natalie said, we really do not have a choice in our current situation."

Karen spoke up, "Effective professional development for our staff means letting go of some of our ego and allowing others to flourish. Dare I say that our staff should have voice and choice in what and how their professional development journey unfolds? Jane, can you share what the task force came up within the other three quadrants?"

"Sure," Jane replied, "In the lower right quadrant, there is professional development that is compliance-based. In this quadrant, we, or someone in our position, is checking the box to verify that training occurred. There is no alignment of the professional development with the vision of the school, the skills needed to make the vision happen, or a strategy on the best method of delivery for the professional development. Think of Rob's experience on his first day as a teacher, and you get a picture of what professional development looks like in this quadrant."

> ## QUOTE
>
> The training they are doing may address an immediate need, but a series of immediate needs don't necessarily equal a long-term plan for change.

Jane continued, "The next quadrant is in the upper right corner of the matrix. This quadrant is the loosey-goosey training that occurs in schools at times. This quadrant is exemplified by training where teachers have voice and choice, they feel empowered, but there is no long-term impact for the school or the participants themselves. A school could easily go through years of this kind of training fooling themselves that the staff is empowering change only to discover the entire school is running in place. The training they are doing may address an immediate need, but a series of immediate needs won't necessarily equal a long-term plan for change.

Without proper reflection on the part of our leadership team, we may get stuck in the quadrant and feel as if we are progressing toward our change goals. Be careful! Unless there are long-term goals and outcomes associated with the training, then we are not going to see contin-ued progress towards The New Learning Ecosystem during the crisis."

Rob thought he knew where Jane was going with her explanation of this quadrant, but he wanted to be sure. "Can we tap the brakes here a lit-tle bit and talk more about this quadrant?" he asked. "You said something to the effect that professional development in this quadrant may satisfy an immediate need, or a series of immediate needs, of the school, but not have a long-term impact. Can you explain that a little bit more?"

"Sure!" she said. "I believe it is so important, and our task force agreed, that professional development needs to explicitly lead to the skills and knowledge needed to reach the long-term goal of the district. The impor-tant word is explicit. Teachers want to know the 'why' of their profes-sional development. Yes, they must believe they have efficacy and choice, but their empowerment only comes when we, as a leadership team, artic-ulate the nexus between the school's vision, the skills and knowledge needed to get there, and teacher empowerment. Without the connection of those three things, our professional development will be stuck in this quadrant. We simply cannot afford to spend any time in this quadrant while we work our way through this crisis."

Karen raised her hand and said, "I can see where this is more than just hanging our vision on a wall. I think it will be important to reinforce with the staff the importance of The New Learning Ecosystem and recon-nect them with the vision. Remind them how important the vision of becoming radically learner-centered is for our learners. Also, remind them how their lives will be better in our school community after they gain the skills."

Rob finished this line of thought with, "I know there is a sense of urgency with all staff because of the COVID-19 crisis. Now is the perfect time to really align the three parts Karen talked about: the vision, the skills, and the knowledge needed to reach the goal of teacher empower-ment. I think all of you have virtual faculty meetings scheduled this week. Let's start the process with our staff by reiterating our long-term vision and how important they are to reaching the vision."

Everyone agreed to do just that during their upcoming faculty meet-ings.

> ## MY TWO CENTS
>
> Our staff needs to become evangelical about the changes that will result from professional development and be able to articulate why these changes will make life better for them and their learners.

Jane finished her review of the professional development matrix, "A quadrant that we do not want to find ourselves in is the one in the lower left. I want to be clear with you, it is easy to fall into the trap as a leader to live in this quadrant. After all, we know the vision, we know the skills needed to reach the vision, so we can fall into the trap of efficiency. Efficiency dictates that we just create the programs and services that we know will lead to our vision, make it available to the staff, and they will attend. Simple. Easy. Efficient. No, do not do it! We may be able to prove short-term gains with this type of training, but there will be no long-term, sustained change because the staff has not bought-in to what the training is asking them to do.

We know we are in this quadrant when we hear the whispers in the faculty room of, 'This too shall pass.' We may also hear a teacher say, 'I've been around long enough to know that what goes around comes around, and this initiative will change when a new leader comes in place.' Our staff needs to become evangelical about the changes that will result from professional development and be able to articulate why these changes will make life better for them and their learners. In other words, every staff member can explain the importance of The New Learning Ecosystem and how the training they are undergoing leads to reaching the vision."

"I want to go back to something that Jane just said," said Karen. "This quadrant is sneaky because we are all 'doers' and often it is easier, maybe even more efficient, to do things ourselves. Mix in a little ego that whispers in our ear that we know what the staff needs, and we can find ourselves creating programs for staff that results in something being done to them instead of being with them."

Jane nodded vigorously and said, "Even when working with the professional development task force, there were so many times when I just wanted to say, 'Here is the answer.' However, that defeats the entire reason for the taskforce and creates a sense of dependency. In this crisis, we are even more tempted to play the all-knowing sage. Let's constantly remind ourselves and each other not to do that".

Craig spoke up. "A friend of mine who is a principal told me that when he started an initiative in his school, he held his tongue an entire year while the teacher team met to discuss what they wanted to do. He had to hold himself back from offering the answer because he recognized that the power of empowerment comes from teachers wrestling with the questions and coming up with solutions themselves. In the end, they came up with great ideas, and he believes that would not have happened if he would have intruded with his version of solutions."

"That's the perfect thought to ponder as we take a quick break and regroup. Stretch, go for a walk, or do whatever you need and meet back here in five minutes," Rob said.

BOOK STUDY QUESTIONS FOR CHAPTER 4

1. The How/Why matrix is so important for effective school leadership during a crisis, or at any time. What quadrant do you belong to in the matrix? Where does everyone on your leadership team fall in the matrix?
2. Who are your "Rock Star" teachers?

    a. Once you identify this group, design a series of meetings with them where you lead them through the Design Thinking process as outlined in this chapter.
    b. Have each rock star create a pilot program in their classroom that reflects the work they did in the Design Thinking process.

3. Who are the people you can positively influence?
4. Assess where your school is on the PD matrix.

    a. What can you do to move your professional development to long-term, with a clear focus?

BOOKS

1. Nine Lies about Work: A Freethinking Leader's Guide to the Real World, (2019), by Marcus Buckingham and Ashley Goodal.
2. What got you here won't get you there: How successful people become even more successful. (2007) by Marshall Goldsmith, Mark Reiter

WEB SITES

1. Sir Ken Robinson, Changing Education Paradigms. https://youtu.be/zDZFcDGpL4U

STAY TRUE TO YOUR STAFF

RESOURCES, MOTIVATION, STRATEGY

"The best way to predict the future is to create it."

—PETER DRUCKER

CHAPTER 5 CONCEPTS AND THINK-ABOUTS

1. Make sure your staff has the resources to fulfill the school's vision
2. Recognizing (and honoring) the Implementation Dip
3. The Results by Design process

PRINCIPLE #4 RESOURCES

THE TEAM FILED back into the conference room and organized themselves around the table. Everyone looked refreshed and eager to keep working on the Crisis Leadership Matrix.

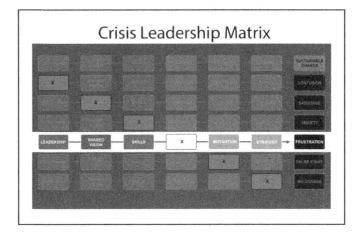

Rob spoke up, "Before we took a break, Craig gave us a perfect segue into the next characteristic on the change matrix—'resources.' It seems we need to make sure the staff has the resources necessary to reach our vision."

Rob looked over at Brett who shook his head in amusement because he knew what was coming and said, "I guess what I am saying Brett, is that we are going to have to open up the checkbook a little bit!"

Brett chuckled. "I'm shocked," he said, with a mildly amused layer of sarcasm.

> ## QUOTE
>
> We cannot count on the charity of our staff. We must make resources available for our teachers to help them be successful.

Rob continued, "A study published in May 2018 showed that an average public-school teacher spends $479 a year on classroom supplies for their learners. Teachers do this because they want what is best for their learners. Whether that's buying tissues or pencils and paper, teachers want their learners prepared to learn. I can remember purchasing novels for my history classes when I was a teacher. Teachers purchasing supplies makes us feel good about the people in front of our kids in school. It shows they are motivated to help our learners. However, school leaders cannot count on the charity of the staff.

We must make resources available for our teachers to help them be successful."

TECHNOLOGY RESOURCES

KAREN, RAISED HER voice to be heard above Rob's, said, "When people don't have the resources needed to complete a job they are asked to accomplish, they get frustrated. A frustrated workforce is not what we want as we work our way through this crisis. There is frustration enough with the massive disruption they are experiencing in their personal and professional life. Let's not hamstring them by not giving them enough resources. There are a few obvious thoughts that come to mind when I think of what our teachers need as resources when it comes to our current crisis situation. I've been thinking about one category of resources in particular since Rob put the matrix on the screen."

Karen continued, "I want to talk about technology as a resource. Before getting excited about the newest whiz-bang piece of technology and thinking about buying it for our staff, we should ask two questions. These questions are particularly important during a crisis.

1. First, does the technology address an actual problem we are trying to solve? I don't know about you, but when I'm reviewing a piece of technology, I often get caught up in what the technology can do, and I lose my original reason for looking at the technology. We must be careful that technology does not become a solution looking for a problem to solve.
2. Second, does the technology do what I need it to do? It is a related question, but one that has to be answered separately from the first one."

Everyone saw that Rob started fidgeting in his seat—an obvious sign he had a story to tell. "I was just talking to a superintendent friend of mine about this very problem," he began. "Last week, her school district brainstormed ideas of how they could get instruction in front of the kids during these times of school buildings being closed. She thought it was a great conversation. They went so far as to put a purchase order together for over $100,000 to buy a certain type of tablet for the learners. They chose the tablet because it was less expensive than some other options, had some preloaded software they knew kids could use, and were available to purchase right away. She is an outstanding leader, so before she signed the purchase order, she gathered the team back together and reviewed their decision-making process. What they discovered was that they did, in fact, get caught up in the capabilities of the tablet, and they became so excited by the perceived capabilities, it turned off the executive part of their brain. They discovered a huge problem with their perfect solution: the cellular broadband service the tablets used for connectivity did not work in their area. They came close to buying the most expensive bricks in the history of the school district. The team quickly made the adjustment to a slightly more expensive solution that would actually work in their area."

Natalie could relate well with this problem because she was friends with the superintendent that almost purchased these technology "bricks." Her friend came close to making a career-ending decision. She chimed in, "Let's be aware of this lesson as we move through the next few weeks and agree to not make any rash decisions about technology!" The group nodded in agreement, looking a little anxious about the "bricks" looming in their future.

NON-TECHNOLOGY RESOURCES

"I ALSO WANT to talk about non-technology resources," Karen started back up again. "In our situation right now, with kids and teachers being forced to stay at home, technology is top of mind. However, we must consider the resources teachers need to create and deliver great instruction. Yes, a lot of that is centered on technology, but it's not the only resource that will help teachers in normal times or in times of crisis. We also must consider intellectual resources. These are resources that teachers need to help expand their knowledge. In our current situation, I think we will need to focus on helping teachers with the nuts and bolts of how to teach in an online environment. I call this 'process knowledge.' If the school buildings stay closed for a longer time, let's keep in mind that teacher's process knowledge is also an important area to grow."

Rob unabashedly decreed as he stood up behind his chair, that he is getting on his proverbial soapbox to pontificate—and that they should all get comfortable. This happened often enough that the leadership team was used to it. They took the moment to unwrap a snack, grab a drink, or settle deeper into their swivel chairs.

He launched into his speech, "What we have discussed so far is the standard definition of resources. These are things that are made available to someone to help them perform a task. I believe that if we want to create rock star leaders, we must expand the definition of what resources are. Specifically, let's think of resources in two different ways.

1. First, our staff is a resource. There is an underlying assumption throughout our conversation today that we must empower staff and learn to give up just a little bit of control so everyone can help reach the school district's goals. This assumption leads to the conclusion that we must check our ego at the door every day. 'To learn, we must accept that we do not know everything.' A simple yet profound statement. We do not want to become like some of my superintendent friends who can't learn anything because they know it all already.

2. Our staff is the best resource to help us get through this crisis. Let's just look at the economics of it. Typically, the salary and benefits of our staff account for 75-80% of our budget. In a strict dollar and sense calculation, we must ask ourselves how we can get the most out of this investment. A school board member once came up to me after a meeting and said something interesting. We had just hired ten new teachers. He looked at me and said, 'Well, the school district just approved a $30 million-dollar investment. Approximately 3 million dollars per teacher over the course of a thirty-year career.' Think about that! It seems that a wise use of the money spent on the staff is to learn from them and allow them to help shape your vision."

Natalie eagerly jumped into the conversation again, "I have been working with the staff on creating curriculum programs for years. Beyond the pure economics of the situation, consider the fact that our staff are the experts interacting with learners, their parents, and the community every day. They may not even realize it, but they have formed expertise about the school and community that is priceless as we figure out how to become radically learner-centered. Besides, who else knows better what they need to help make the necessary changes to help us through this crisis? This is not to say those of us sitting around this table will not have a say in the shape of reaching the school district's goals. The role of all of us sitting around the table is to create a shared understanding of the possibilities and any limitations related to resource creation. We get to structure a conversation with teachers that helps them understand the bigger picture of what is being achieved. They help with how to get it done. When this happens, the alignment of resources occurs."

Brett spoke up, "Before anyone starts looking at me out of the corner of your eye, let's get something straight. We joke around about me holding the purse strings tight because I am the business manager of the school district. I go along with the joking myself. I want to make sure everyone around this table understands something important: I am as committed to The New Learning Ecosystem as anyone else sitting at this table.

Sure, I take my job of being fiscally responsible seriously, but so does everyone else here. I have a deeper knowledge of the rules, regulations, and policies that prop up our budget, and I want to use them to the best effect possible to help the school district get through the COVID-19 crisis and reach our goals of becoming radically learner-centered."

Rob nodded in agreement and said, "I have a dear friend that says a budget can support any initiative you want to undertake if you have the flexibility to move money around. So, for example, you may move money from supplies to professional development in one year because that is where the best use of the money can be used. Maybe in the following year, you do just the opposite as the training the staff received in year one required an influx of resources. Whatever the case, we need to have the courage and creativity to view the budget as a living document.

> ## QUOTE
>
> Does our budget reflect the values of our school?

There is a saying that a budget reflects the values of the organization. Does our budget reflect the values of our school? In the upcoming weeks and months, will people be able to look at the financial decisions we make and be able to decipher our values based on how we use the budget? I hope so."

PRINCIPLE #5 MOTIVATION

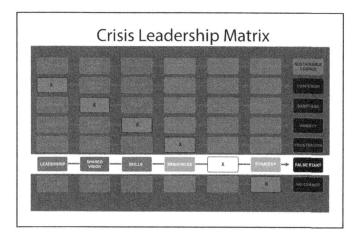

"As I look at the change matrix on the wall, I see that if we don't have the next characteristic, then we will experience false starts in the change process," Jane offered. "We simply cannot afford to have a false start in the work of getting through this crisis. In our new leadership reality of VUCA, false starts will mean that we do not accomplish what we need to accomplish. The question we will have to ask ourselves and our staff is whether or not we really believe we can make the change. Our staff did not just go home on vacation when the Governor closed the school buildings. Overnight, they became work from home experts expected to deliver great instruction to our kids in a fashion they have never worked in before: the online environment. In addition to all of that, there is the little fact that we are in the middle of a pandemic. They know people who are sick, they can't visit their elderly relatives, some of them even have their own kids home and are trying to manage that. The question of motivation is key."

Karen picked up on Jane's train of thought: "I also think that we have an incredible amount of motivation right now because of the crisis. Our staff wants to get back to interacting with learners in the most meaningful way possible. A sense of urgency has been created for us—we don't have to worry about strategizing how to help people get a sense of urgency. We have laid the groundwork for The New Learning Ecosystem vision, and the vision is helping build motivation".

> ## My Two Cents
>
> 3 steps to keep motivation high within your staff.
>
> 1. Talk about, and honor, the implementation dip
> 2. Create your own indicators of success that let you know what success looks like when your school becomes radically learner-centered.
> 3. Make failure survivable. The best way to do this is to have small, pilot programs spread throughout your school and school district.

"I want to piggyback on Karen's thoughts," added Craig as he placed his bottle of water on the table in front of him. "There is something vital that we have to get on the table when we talk about motivation and that is: does our staff have the motivation to fight through the difficulties that will arise as we double down on our vision during this crisis? In normal times, we know we have to pay attention to motivation. Motivation lags when complexity enters the picture. That's in normal times. Now that we are in a VUCA world, the complexity and uncertainty are magnified. We talked earlier about making sense of the world for our staff members. What are the ways we can help make sense of the world to keep motivation high?"

Natalie was the first to answer. "We need to talk about the implementation dip. Any organizational system takes time to adjust to the new way of doing things—and performance dips before it gets better. In a way, we are fortunate because, most of the time, a crisis throws an organization into a dip in performance anyway. Think about what teachers are doing right now. We changed from a well-run, functioning, brick-and-mortar school to an online school overnight! We are in an implementation dip right now. Hopefully, we are at the bottom of the dip, but chances are we aren't."

Craig replied, "Maybe it's a blessing in disguise that we are in an implementation dip forced by the crisis. The fear of failure is not as strong as the motivation to do something different to help the learners."

"I agree," Natalie continued, "Let's be upfront with everyone about the implementation dip from the outset. Let our staff, students, and parents know that things may continue to get worse before they get better. I think to mitigate the negative consequences of the implementation dip, we must do one thing: create a list of indicators of success that will help people see whether our school is successfully reaching our goals to become radically learner-centered in the current crisis.

Because of the work we have done in the past two years, we've answered the important question around indicators of success, which is 'What does success look like for our school district when it becomes radically learner-centered?' The long-term vision has not changed. Since we're in a major crisis, we should create short-term indicators of success that are aligned with and cascade into the long-term indicators of success. Now, we usually would have a thorough strategic design process to help us develop the indicators of success. Obviously, that can't happen in our current crisis."

This inspired Karen and she spoke up. "We can explain our understanding of the current reality, which is the VUCA world. We also need to discuss the challenge of transforming into an online school and the opportunities the crisis offers to become radically learner-centered. I think we'll need to reach out to our contacts in the community on an individual basis and get their input that way. We can discuss our thinking at our faculty meetings too. Between these two methods, we will get good feedback. At that point in time, our team sitting around the table here can create the short-term indicators of success. After they are created, it's imperative that we communicate them to the school community. Not only will you share the new indicators of success, but by sharing the new indicators, you can start to tell the story of why the changes are necessary. It'll also show that we are not abandoning our vision for the school, and we are being proactive to accelerate reaching the vision."

"One last thought," Karen added. "It's an important one: make failure survivable. There will be days ahead when what we thought would work will be an utter and complete failure. That's all right. There is no failure if you learn from experience and adjust and change to make it better. Especially in the world we live in right now, with the implementation dip so steep, it will help make some of the mistakes not to look so bad. Small failures will not change our destination, the failures simply change the route we use to reach our destination. Acknowledging up front that we know there will be some things that won't work helps keep people from giving up after something goes wrong. Letting people know that a small failure only means that we now know what not to do is important to keep motivation high."

The leadership team was excited and exhausted at the same time—excited because they saw the possibilities and exhausted because the past three weeks have been mentally, emotionally, and physically draining. They had a big job ahead of them and it was obvious everyone felt the weight of that task.

"I think it will also help keep motivation high if we can corral failure into small areas," Rob said. "When we work with our rock stars, let's approach them with a 'pilot program' mentality. I have seen this pilot program idea work wonders in schools. Let's take advantage of the people that get excited for change and have them show their colleagues that what we are asking them to do will help the school community through this crisis and help reach our goal of becoming radically learner-centered. Most of our staff will want to 'see it in action' before they are going to fully commit to making the changes. Because there is such an acute sense of urgency in our current situation, the motivation of the rock star teachers to want to do something, and the motivation of the karaoke stars to want to see something positive will be high." ...

That meeting was three years ago but it still holds great meaning for Rob. He's brought back to the present day as he finds himself pulling into the parking lot to his office. Isn't it funny, he thinks to himself, how our mind allows us to wander as it performs routine tasks? The mind lets us function through actions that are habits, like driving back to the office, while thinking about other things. He started to think about the meeting at a stoplight not far from his office and now finds himself at his office. Looking back, he can barely remember driving through town!

He pulls into his parking place, shuts down the car, and takes a deep breath. Rob's spent a lot of time over the last few years sharing the school district's experience during the COVID-19 crisis. He shakes his head in wonder when he realizes he learns something new about his experience during the COVID-19 crisis whenever he shares the story. As he opens the door to get out of the car, the smell of the flowers planted outside the office building brings a memory back to him. He thinks back to the walk behind his office in the early days of the COVID-19 crisis and the effect the sighting of the red-winged blackbird had on him. In a lot of ways, it was a transformational event in his professional career.

PRINCIPLE #6 STRATEGY

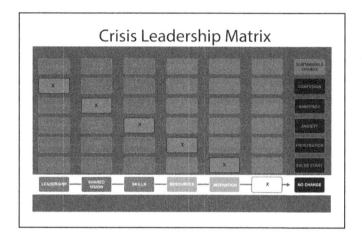

Shutting the door to his car and walking to his office, Rob remembers the one area in the complex change matrix that he knows was the weakest for himself and the leadership team during the COVID-19 crisis: strategy.

He doesn't know if strategy was a weakness because of the crisis or whether strategy is a systemic weakness in his leadership repertoire. Even during the height of the crisis, there was a sense that he couldn't shake that he and the leadership team were not paying enough attention to strategy. The justification he gave to himself for the lack of attention was because things were moving so quickly that there was no time for "strategy." They were in survival mode, after all. Fortunately, the team paid just enough attention to strategy that the changes they wanted to accomplish were achieved. Opening the door to his office complex, Rob knows that the next time a crisis comes, they might not be so lucky with strategy. They are going to have to be more purposeful about it. As a matter of fact, Rob has retooled his entire strategic design process to make sure strategy is not just something to check on a compliance document, but something embedded in the strategic design process itself.

"Hello Rob. How was your meeting with Kermit? Did you have the western omelet?" asks Elaine, his administrative assistant.

"You can probably guess the answer to that question," Rob answers. "Yes, for the latter question, and you know that telling our school district story energizes me, especially when I am talking to someone that wants to change the world, so talking to Kermit was awesome."

"That's wonderful! Right before you came in, Don called. He shared with me how much he and their school board appreciated your work with them during their strategic design process. He does want you to call him, though. He has a question about solidifying next steps for his district in their strategic design," Elaine says.

"The timing couldn't be better; I was just thinking about that very topic." Rob takes the message from Elaine's in-box and walks into his office to call Don.

This is what Rob has learned since going through the COVID-19 crisis: next to leadership, strategy is the most important aspect to consider on the crisis change management matrix. If there is no strategy, no change will occur. The second effect of having no strategy, other than the fact that you will not see any change, is resentment. Your staff wants to know that there is a plan for how you are implementing learner-centered change. Even more than having knowledge that there is, in fact, a plan, they want to be a part of the plan. To contribute to something larger than themselves. To have a voice in their school. Both of these types of participation come from carefully planning a strategy.

Rob thinks of a conversation he recently had with a central office school administrator to talk about changes they wanted to make in their school district. This person had put a lot of thought into the change they wanted to make. They had well-thought-out reasons for the change. The school district considered the changes in the systems that needed to be adjusted. They had even thought about the people that needed to make the change. Rob was excited for them. He then asked a simple question, "what is your implementation strategy?" They answered, "Oh, we are going to do it next year."

"Next year?" Rob asked incredulously.

"Yes, I will just tell them to do it!" they said.

This was an obvious recipe for disaster. The changes they wanted to make will take a minimum of five years to achieve. School leaders vastly underestimate the time it will take to make systemic changes in their system. Their underestimation is a result of not including staff members and the wider school community in the discussions from the start. You do not have to have community meetings to decide what to do, (another recipe for disaster, from Rob's experience) but once you make a case for the changes, the community must be involved in the how of the change.

Rob gets tired of leaders who view a strategic design simply as a compliance document—a process you must complete because someone (the State, The Feds, or your school board) wants you to do it. Rob also gets frustrated that people make the strategic design process too complicated. Rob has a simple motto when it comes to strategy: keep it simple.

RESULTS BY DESIGN

ROB USES RESULTS by Design©. Results by Design© is a strategic design process developed specifically for school districts by the Pennsylvania Leadership Development Center. This process uses "design thinking," which helps groups think outside of the box while relentlessly focusing on the experience of the end-user of a product or service. The design thinking process is popular in Silicon Valley. Rob has taken pieces of each system to create a strategic design process that focuses on implementation.

Rob reaches for his phone and dials Don's number. It's not uncommon for people to get a little panicked as they look at starting their change process, and he suspects that Don is feeling some anxiety.

Don answers the phone, and Rob greets him with, "Hello Don, how is everything going for you today?"

"Not too bad," answers Don. "Since you were here two months ago, we have started putting into action the work to make the strategic design come alive for our school district. Things seem to be going relatively well."

"I knew your school and community would wrap their arms around the vision they created. However, I can't help but hear some worry in your voice. What's going on?" Rob asks.

"Is it that obvious that I am staring at the panic button and wanting to hit it really hard?" Don replies. "I'll be honest, the night we finished our strategic design, I was so pumped up I could hardly get to sleep that night. It was almost like a runner's high. I just love our purpose, mission, and vision. Right when I am feeling good, I start to think about every-thing that needs to be done to reach our goals, and some doubt creeps in."

"The feeling of doubt is natural, and it happens when you focus too much on the long-term goals and not the present moment," Rob answers. "So, let's look back at what you have done with your school community, how you did it, how an implementation strategy is embedded in the work, and why you don't need to worry so much."

Rob continues, "Remember that we used a combination of the design thinking process and the Results by Design© process. We use this method because it engrains an implementation strategy into the strategic design process. So, remember, there are five parts to the process: discovery, inter-pretation, ideation, experimentation, and evolution. Each part of the process is grounded in a question that guides the work.

We started with getting together with key stakeholders in the com-munity—the people that the school needed to hear from. I really like this beginning part because it is so laser-focused on the ideal future of the school. We wanted to answer these five questions and create succinct statements based on the answers:

- Purpose—why do we exist?
- Beliefs/Values—what do we believe and value?
- Mission—what do we do?
- Vision—what does the organization look like when it is at its ideal best?
- Indicators of Success—what do we measure?

The purpose of these tabletop discussions was to create the purpose, value, mission, and vision statements as if your school was operating fifteen years in the future. The statements that resulted from this exercise were fantas-tic. The group placed a stake in the ground that was just far enough ahead of you so you could see it, but you would have to work to get there."

"I remember that night well," answers Don. "Those statements are just coming off the printer now. We will have them out in the schools and community soon. I appreciate you reminding me of that night. Although it was only two months ago, so much has changed in our school district since then. Not so much that you can see what the changes are, the change is in the hope and excitement about the future. Instead of dreading the future, we are embracing the future."

"Don't forget," Rob reminds Don, "the group decided that first night that cascading the goals was important. Aligning the vision of your individual schools with the vision of the school district was viewed as an important activity. Every school is unique in its strengths and challenges and developing purpose, values, mission, and vision for every school that reflects their uniqueness while at the same time aligning to the district's goals is important."

"I loved it when you looked at our business manager and Board president when the group decided on this course of action and said, 'Are you going to put your money where your mouth is?

MY TWO CENTS

A simple way to embed a school district's vision and goals throughout the entire school system:

1. Create school district-wide vision statements, goal statements, and indicators of success.
2. Each school creates their own vision statement, goal statement, and indicators of success that encompass the school district's vision.
3. Employee goals for the year align to the school's vison statements, goal statements and indicators of success.

Because if you're not, we should all just leave right now. The group just decided to invite all teachers to come into their schools for one day in the summer and create their purpose, values, mission, and vision statement...and you have to pay them for that time!' You could have heard a pin drop for the nano-second it took them to both say 'yes' at the same time!" Don recalls.

Rob laughs at the memory. "Just to let you know, I prepped them for just such a question beforehand so I knew what their answer was going to be...or at least I was pretty confident they would say yes!"

"They're good people and dedicated to leading the district into the future, so I am sure it was an easy question for them to answer," Don says.

Rob continues, "The last part of the evening was easier, the group had to develop a design challenge to serve as the basis for the rest of the process which centered on implementation. We designed the entire strategic design process to make sure implementation was baked into the process. Your design challenge, 'How might we structure our learning community to meet the unique needs of every learner?' is powerful. Are you any less anxious now?"

"Yeah, I am," says Don. I can picture your first slide talking about the discovery process when we met with the rock star teacher group. You had a big outline of all the steps we had to follow to get the rock stars engaged..."

DESIGN THINKING

Discovery:

Our challenge today is to answer this question:

How might we structure our learning community to meet the unique needs of every learner?

Step 1:

- Form small groups. Make sure you are not sitting with your friends from the same school!
- Discussion #1: What will our school, community, and society look like in fifteen years? Thirty years?
- Video: TED talk with Sir Ken Robinson titled Changing the Education Paradigm.
- How can our school become the ideal that Robinson talks about in the video? What needs to change in our systems and structures?
- Everyone needs to then create your own design problem that will help answer the school district's design challenge. Begin your design challenge with the question "how might we...".

Step 2: Now you have a problem to solve.

- Research your problem in the real world.
- This includes observations, interviews, questionnaires, and focus groups...

Don comes out of his trance as he stares out his office window thinking back to the work with the rock star teachers and says, "This was a key part of the design thinking process—getting out into the real world to observe what is actually going on. We had teachers shadow students, interview politicians, and do various activities to really understand the context of their specific problem. By doing this, the teachers understood they were not going to create something that was just an intellectual exercise, rather it had practical usefulness. We gave them two weeks to do their 'observation' homework'"

"Yes, it was 2 weeks," Rob answers, "and I always like the next part of the process because I love to hear the stories the teachers tell after they had gone out and done their research." Rob looks at his whiteboard in his office where his ideas from his brainstorming session for Don are still visible.

Interpretation:

Guiding question: "I learned something, how do I interpret it?"

"In some ways, this was the most fun part of the process for me. By working in groups, teachers shared their learnings and conceptualized what they learned in the context of reimagining schools. This part of the process led to a much more focused individual design challenge, based on real-world observations and experiences. The next two parts of the design thinking process helped the teachers refine their design challenge and make it practical for their school and classrooms."

Ideation:

Guiding Question: "I see an opportunity, what do I create?"

Don recalls, "I helped you facilitate this part of the process since it requires so much mental 'heavy lifting.' Working in groups, teachers used the information learned from the first two parts of the process and started to brainstorm ideas of what they could do in their classrooms or school setting to solve their design challenge. Ideas had to be completed within the next three months. This time limitation encouraged creativity by focusing the participants on small, doable projects—the best way to encourage grassroots change, in my opinion. If you don't mind, Rob, I am going to spit out what I remember of the next stage of experimentation."

Rob encourages him to continue. He knows that the more Don recalls the process, the less anxious he'll feel.

Experimentation:

Guiding question: "I have an idea; how do I build it?"

Don continues, "Teachers then took the idea they created and applied it to the real world. I encouraged teachers to approach this section with a pilot program mentality. They used an idea with the understanding that parts of their idea will likely need to be changed. This was the iterative process in action. Failure is accepted as progress toward the desired innovation. This lessened the anxiety of teachers who often are afraid to make mistakes and seek to be perfect all the time. As we adopted it, the design thinking process encourages rapid iteration of ideas as participants learn what works, what does not work, and the base changes on what's being learned."

"Now, stop right there," Rob says. "This is where you are right now. Teachers are out there implementing their ideas. Enjoy the process. We stressed to them that some of the stuff they wanted to do would work and other things would not. That's fine and to be expected. They have one more month of their pilot projects. Go out and see what they are doing and enjoy their stories of success and near-success."

Rob finishes, "As a matter of fact, the last phase of the process anticipates that there will be changes in almost everybody's design challenge. The old saying, 'a battle plan never survives first contact with the enemy' is important to remember."

"I remember you saying that to the team. We have our 'evolution' session planned for six weeks from now," Don answers.

Evolution:

Guiding question: "I tried something new, how do I evolve it?"

Once a participant iterated a design challenge solution as a pilot program in the experimentation phase, the teachers then come back together and share what they learn. They will first meet in their original groups to get feedback from those colleagues that are most familiar with their project. The next step is to create new groups so teachers will have to explain their design challenge pilot program with people that are not familiar with it. This feedback is important because it will come from people who also had gone through a similar experience creating and modifying their own ideas.

"So, I hope our talk has walked you back from the edge, Don," Rob says. "You and your school district have done the foundational work to make lasting change in your schools. Just keep track of your strategy. Move the work from the rock star teachers to the karaoke stars and begin to deal with the no stars. There will be trials and tribulations along the way, but you will get through them. I am confident of that."

"This talk has been a great help, thank you," Don answers. "I'm not looking over the abyss anymore and the panic button is nowhere in sight. I'll let you know how our meeting with the rock star teachers goes when I meet with them in a month."

"I look forward to it," Rob answers.

As he hung up the phone, Rob reflected on his leadership journey that started the day the Governor closed all of the school buildings in the State. What he learned through those times has informed much of his leadership style today. He certainly does not wish for another crisis the level of the COVID-19 crisis, but he believes the school district, his leadership team, the staff, and learners are in a better place because of what everyone learned as they made their way through the crisis. Rob stares out the window looking out over the school property and watches a red-winged blackbird land on a branch. Rob can't hear the bird's song, but he knows the tune. Rob's proud of the work his schools and community have accomplished. Life is good.

BOOK STUDY QUESTIONS FOR CHAPTER 5

1. What are the two principles in the Crisis Leadership Matrix that are the most well-developed for you and your school? How will you leverage these strengths?
2. Send a series of newsletters to your school's stakeholders explaining the school's vision, mission, and goals. Use examples from your school showing how the vision, mission, and goals are being implemented in your school.

BOOKS

1. Results By Design: A Field book for Planning by Duff Rearick, et al.
2. Dare to Lead: Brave Work, Tough Conversations. Whole Hearts, (2018) by Brene Brown.
3. The 5TH Discipline: The Art and Practice of The Learning Organization, (2006), by Peter Senge.
4. Fierce Conversations: Achieving Success at Work and Life, One Conversation at a Time, (2004), by Susan Scott.

WEB SITES

1. Design Thinking Resource *https://designthinking.ideo.com/*
2. Sir Ken Robinson, Changing Education Paradigms. *https://youtu.be/zDZFcDGpL4U*
3. The Future of Learning by 2Revolutions. *https://youtu.be/JcMWavvD5xI*
4. What is Design Thinking. *https://youtu.be/a7sEoEvT8l8*

EPILOGUE

"C OME ON IN and have a seat," Rob waves Scott, the School Board President, to a chair in his office as he closes the door behind them. "What is on your mind today Scott?"

Rob suspects he knows the answer to this question. Not too long after helping Don's school district with its strategic design process, their superintendent position became available. Although Rob was not looking to change jobs, the idea intrigues him.

"I bet you can guess why I'm here," Scott begins as he sits on the edge of the chair. "I heard rumors that our neighbors to the west have been recruiting you for their open superintendent position. I just wanted to come in and talk confidentially with you about the rumors. I know I speak for the Board when I say that we have appreciated your leadership throughout the last eight years. You have helped the community create a vision and get behind the vision. Of course, your work through the COVID-19 crisis was exemplary."

"Thank you for those kind words Scott," Rob answers. "It has been a blast working with the Board, the staff, the community, and the kids over the past eight years. I have been blessed to work with such great people. I have enough respect for you and the school community to be upfront and honest with you about the job with our friends to the west."

Rob has been anticipating this conversation for a while. Although he has not applied for the other school district's job, he has been approached by representatives of the school district asking him if he is interested. He has been told that he is their number one choice for the job.

Rob continues, "The school district has approached me, and they want me to talk to them about their open position. I learned a lot about the district when I helped them with their strategic design. Their community is excited about their new vision, and I see a lot of potential in their school and community. I know their Board wants to talk to me because they know of the work we all did together in this district to guarantee a radically learner-centered school system."

"We have come a long way in this district in five years, that's for sure." Scott leans back in his chair as he answers. "The connections the school has built with our community, and the learning experiences that are being created for our learners is inspiring. I just want you to think of one thing...your work here is not done. I, and the Board, are so proud of how far we have come by embracing The New Learning Ecosystem, and we do not want to lose momentum. We know it is difficult to keep momentum when the leader leaves the district."

"I understand where you are coming from on that last point, Scott," replies Rob, "but I know that Jane is ready to step in and help facilitate all of the changes that are necessary to keep the school district on track. Plus, you have heard me say this a thousand times, my goal was to make our changes 'leader proof'. Once we have the systems and structures embedded in the school, it will not matter who is at the helm. The system will continue to run. That is the beauty of our strategic design and our vision. You know that I am an authentic leader. I believe in empowering the learners and the staff. Our structures and systems have changed to support our vision. Think about it, if COVID-19 couldn't derail us, what can?"

"I get it, Rob. And I agree that Jane will make a great superintendent because she is an outstanding leader. I am also the Board president, and I have the best interest of the school district in mind, and right now, we believe the best interest of the school district means you are staying with us." Scott answers.

Rob looks around his office at all of the mementos of his time in the district. Pictures of learners, posters of school musicals, and framed copies of the school district's vision remind him how blessed he is to work for the school district. He replies to Scott, "All great points. I have not committed to even talking to them yet, so you know where I am as of today. I love this district, and the thought of leaving after everything we have accomplished together is gut-wrenching." Rob winces when he finishes the sentence. He has a love for the district and the people in the community that is unrivaled.

"That settles it," Scott says, "You'll stay with us!"

Rob laughs and says, "We'll see. This is a hard decision, and you will be the first to know if I get any closer to making a decision."

Made in United States
North Haven, CT
07 June 2022

19970380R00104